BWB Texts

Short books on big subjects from
great New Zealand writers

The Best of e-Tangata

EDITED BY TAPU MISA
AND GARY WILSON

Published in 2017 by Bridget Williams Books Limited, PO Box 12474, Wellington 6144, New Zealand, www.bwb.co.nz, info@bwb.co.nz.

All of the pieces in this book have been previously published on *e-Tangata*. They are reproduced here as first published, with some light editing.

ISBN 9780947518455 (Paperback), ISBN 9780947518462 (EPUB)
ISBN 9780947518479 (Kindle), ISBN 9780947518486 (PDF)
DOI 10.7810/9780947518455

A catalogue record for this book is available from the National Library of New Zealand. Kei te pātenga raraunga o Te Puna Mātauranga o Aotearoa te whakarārangi o tēnei pukapuka

Acknowledgements
The publisher acknowledges the ongoing support provided by the Bridget Williams Books Publishing Trust and Creative New Zealand.

ARTS COUNCIL OF NEW ZEALAND TOI AOTEAROA

Publisher: Tom Rennie
Editors: Geoff Walker and Anna Hodge
Cover and internal design: Base Two
Typesetter: Tina Delceg
Printer: Printlink, Wellington

CONTENTS

INTRODUCTION

When we launched the *e-Tangata* website in late 2014, there were those who asked us why we were bothering. Why did New Zealand need another magazine dedicated to Māori and Pasifika stories and commentary? What could we provide that was any different from what was already there?

We confess that our first reaction was exasperation. We hope this collection does a better job of answering those questions.

These days, there *is* more Māori and Pasifika journalism about. But *e-Tangata* provides something different. For a start it brings together, on one site (in a largely *pro bono* venture), the observations of many of our sharpest writers and thinkers. And it does so through a Māori, Pasifika and Pākehā team who see a need for a concerted effort to reflect the whole range of New Zealand society.

For both of us, this is just the latest chapter in a decades-long effort to ensure that the stories that feed and shape the national consciousness – and the voices that contribute to national conversations – aren't just those supplied to us by a mainstream media that still struggles to see and hear beyond its white borders.

As the poet Muriel Rukeyser wrote: 'The universe is made of stories, not of atoms.' And if we're to remake Aotearoa New Zealand into a country where all of us, no matter what our whakapapa, can thrive and feel at ease with one another, then our stories and our voices need to be part of that universe.

Our stories should not only reflect us – in all our many splendoured ways – they should light the way, too.

Our stories help us to make sense of who we are and who we want to be. By telling our stories, we're bringing others into our world. This is vitally important in an age where growing inequality heightens divisions and widens the distances between us.

We hope that by sharing our stories, our ways of thinking, our experiences, our hopes and dreams, we will not only break down the ignorance that divides us – as described with such rare courage and honesty by Andrew Judd in his interview with Dale Husband – but also inspire and help others to rub the cultural sleep from their eyes, as Kennedy Warne writes in his evocative piece on Ngāpuhi elder Saana Murray.

This collection is drawn from *e-Tangata*'s first two years. It's a taste of a rich archive of engaging and deeply personal reflections on the experience of living in Aotearoa – from Māori, Pasifika and Pākehā. As the website grows, we hope to include more from others who make their home in this part of the world.

One of *e-Tangata*'s particular strengths has been the illuminating Q&A interviews by Dale Husband (Ngāti Maru, Pākehā), whose warmth and empathy has allowed us to present the stories of a wide range of New Zealanders in their own voices.

A few of them are included here.

Eliota Fuimaono-Sapolu, a lawyer and former Manu Samoa player whose complaints about the colonial version of New Zealand and Pacific history he was taught at Auckland Grammar broke our site (and still holds the record for our most-read piece with 130,000 unique views).

Ngāpuhi kaumātua Kingi Taurua, who was known most of his life as Albert, after the family rooster, because, on his first day at school, his teacher sent him home to 'find a Pakeha name'.

Dame Joan Metge, one of many Pākehā repelled by New Zealand's racism, which she first saw in Pukekohe as a schoolgirl in the 1940s.

Gilbert Enoka, the boy from an orphanage who went on to help shape an All Blacks culture based on being a good person.

And Naida Glavish, who made headlines in the 1980s as the tolls operator who dared to greet callers with 'kia ora'.

Naida's story, like many here, reminds us not only of how far we've come – but how far we still have to go.

Ngā mihi. Soifua.
Tapu Misa and Gary Wilson

NAIDA GLAVISH
SHE WOULDN'T COMPLY

In the 1980s, Naida Glavish made headlines as the Post Office tolls operator who was threatened with dismissal for greeting callers with 'kia ora'. She stuck to her guns and won, with help from an unexpected ally. But there's much more to her story than that, as she told Dale Husband in this interview published in September 2015.

Dale Husband: *Well now, Naida. I think we should start with your names because neither of them are at all common here in Aotearoa. The Glavish surname suggests some interesting whakapapa. And your first name is so uncommon that many of us aren't even sure how to pronounce it. Some say* Nayda. *Some say* Nyda. *Some say* Nah-ee-da.

Naida Glavish: Actually, my first name is Rangimarie. I was named by my grandmother on

11

instruction from her father. But it's not 'Rangimarie the peaceful'. It's Rangimarie and Rangi where all the storms happened. And Marie is to be the creator of peace rather than peace itself. So that's my name, but it doesn't get used.

The Naida part of my name is Croatian and some of my Croatian relations tell me that it means hope. So there's hope for peace, I guess. It's actually Nah-ee-da. That's how a Croatian would say it.

But I'll answer to both. It's Naida here nor there.

And the Glavish name?

The Glavish name was originally spelled G-l-a-v-a-s. And it was pronounced Glavash, with the emphasis on the second syllable. My grandmother and grandfather came over to New Zealand from Croatia in nineteen hundred and something and the name got anglicised to Glavish to make it more acceptable here.

Can you tell us about your whānau and your background as a young girl?

I was raised and nurtured on the shores of the Kaipara harbour by a grandmother, Ngapeka Teririkore Nahi (née Panui). I was actually born in the front seat of my father's Studebaker car, as a matter of fact. The family story was that I was probably conceived in the back seat, and that I'd been on the road ever since. But when I raised that subject with my father, all he did was chuckle – and have a laugh about it.

Anyway, I was brought up by my Māori grand-mother, and across the road was the Croatian grandmother, Marija Glavish. Her maiden name was Delich.

Neither grandmother could speak English very well, so I bounced from one to the other – and I had to go to school to learn to speak English properly. We lived in a nīkau whare with an earth floor. It was very clean. I remember once when the public health nurse had to visit (because an aunty was there with her baby) and she was just full of praise about the cleanliness of our whare with the earth floor. Even though it was considered ill-mannered to speak about someone's home, Mama (my grandmother) didn't comment.

So I grew up with the values of tapu and noa, and karakia for everything with my grandmother. Not playing with food. We were raised with the understanding of the pull of the tide for fishing purposes. Understanding the moon hases for planting and growing our kai, the tāpapa for the kūmara and, at the time of harvest for the kūmara, how to prepare the pit with burnt fern leaves so that the slugs couldn't get in, but also preparing a pit with the little kūmara for the slugs, rats and the like so that they didn't go near the pit for our consumption. It was a very rich upbringing really. The birds and the trees and shrubs also had their part to play as our messengers for the crops, and the kai beneath the sea.

Of course, I had to go to school, but I didn't learn much there that was of any use to me that I hadn't already learned at home.

How about those school days?

I was expelled from one school and suspended from two. I was a fluent speaker of two languages, and I had a little knowledge of Croatian from Grandma Glavish. So that tells us how well it worked out.

My first school was at Pukekohe – that racist town of Pukekohe – where, for instance, us Māori weren't allowed to sit upstairs at the picture theatre. I spent a few years there because Mama was a widow and needed to go to Pukekohe to work in the market gardens. I actually attended the Pukekohe Native School. I absolutely enjoyed living with my mama. I was truly loved.

But then I was called back to my mum who'd had twins to my stepdad, a beautiful man from Rarotonga. So when I was called back to my mum, I attended Helensville Primary School and then Helensville High, which has become Kaipara College.

But, being Māori, I was put in the 'B' stream. Never mind that I got only two answers wrong out of a hundred. The 'A' stream wasn't where all the

Māori were. They were 'B'. So that was where I was sent.

And why was it that I didn't get along at school? I suppose you could say that it was just that … well … I didn't comply.

Now, what about your mum?

She was Nohotakitahi, although they called her Nora because the schoolteachers of her time couldn't pronounce Nohotakitahi. She had three of us to Frank Glavish. There was Robert, me, and David. Both my brothers have died. Mum and Frank separated and she then met this wonderful man, Paniani Tapurau, and they married. Mum and Paniani had twin girls, Lucy and Lisa.

So you had a few siblings?

Well, yes, Frank Glavish had nine of us to four different women.

The devil.

Yes, that's Glavish. He died in 2013 aged 101.

Nine kids to four different women. Wow. That could be the secret to longevity.

Well, he would swear by it.

All right. Let's move on from his escapades. Did you get caught up in the urban drift? Did rock 'n' roll lure you into the city?

Oh, yes. I got caught up in the urban drift. When I was living with my grandmother, I was an absolutely loved child. She saw that I didn't want for anything. Clothes, shoes, or anything at all. But my cousin didn't have the luxury of the things I had. She was working in the market gardens and, one time when we were walking home from where she worked, she saw some clothes on a tank stand. So she decided that she would go and claim them – which she did. And she got spotted by some neighbours who rang the police.

She then pleaded with me to say it was me because I wouldn't get a hiding from my grandmother but she surely would from her mother. So I said: 'Yes. It was me.' Even though those things she took wouldn't fit me. Anyway, long story short, I ended up in a courtroom in Pukekohe and then in child welfare for four years. And from the age of twelve to the age of sixteen, I went to ten different homes.

Wow. I find that unimaginable. But, anyway, that was the reality for you. Ten different homes. Just trying to cover for a cousin. That must've been a dark period of your life?

Well, it was. It really was, because, as a twelve-year-old, I was torn from the bosom of this beautiful beloved grandmother of mine. She stood on the footpath as these two social workers, Pākehā women, drove off with her mokopuna in their car into the sunset. She didn't know where they were taking me. Neither did I. It was my first trip ever over the harbour bridge. Then it was ten different homes. I attended Takapuna Grammar and then Northcote College. It was four years of my life where I experienced the Department of Social Welfare at its worst.

Was there abuse?

No. Not for me. No, there wasn't. There was certainly emotional and psychological abuse, but nothing physical.

You're sixteen by now and, I'm assuming, you were finally able to break free of social welfare. How did that come to be?

I don't know. I honestly don't know. They just decided: 'Oh, well. You're sixteen now so you can pack up and go.' Which I did. I went home. I can still remember my sixteenth birthday back home because it was the first time in four years that I was able to come together with all my cousins and Mum and aunties and uncles.

And then what?

I went to work in a sewing factory in Helensville. And I married young. I was only seventeen but I was a mature seventeen. I had six children. I lost one daughter in a tragic accident. I didn't go to work after I married until all my children had gone to school, and when my baby went off to school in 1975, I went back to work. That was as a toll operator.

My beloved grandmother developed a cataract and was blind so I went and brought her to live with me. She taught me so much in her blindness. She was with me when I was having my children.

We don't hear much about your man. Is he around still?

Oh, yeah. We've separated. But he's out at Kaipara. He's well. Between us, we now have nineteen grandchildren: thirteen grandsons and six granddaughters. We also have 22 greats today: twelve great-grandsons and ten great-granddaughters.

Beautiful.

It's called immortality guaranteed.

Lovely. Now let's check out the fuss you caused when, as a phone operator for the Post Office, you dared to say: 'Kia ora, tolls here.' That wasn't the accepted routine, was it? So you could've got the boot.

Well, that was in 1984, some years after my grandmother had died in 1972. And the whole affair was a worry because, if I was to be dismissed for saying 'kia ora', it would've also meant being evicted from the Post Office house that I was renting. So I was thinking that I'd had just about enough of this battle.

Then, as I was driving over the harbour bridge, I heard this voice in my ear: *Nui ake tēnei take i a koe.* (This is far greater than you.) As if to say: 'Who do you think you are?' Anyway, I thought it was the wind whistling through the window so I wound it up. And then it came again. So I knew that my grandmother was telling me that this business was far greater than me – so I went to the supervisor and said: 'You do what you have to do as my supervisor, and I will respect it. But I will do what I have to do as the child of my grandmother.' Then I went back and sat on the toll board and said: 'Kia ora, tolls here.'

Rangi Walker was the then chairman of the Auckland District Māori Council so I rang him and told him that I was being harassed and threatened with dismissal because I said 'kia ora, tolls here' instead of 'good morning' or 'good afternoon'.

Rangi then made a phone call to the New Zealand Māori Council, which was under the chairmanship of Graham Latimer, who supported the idea that the Post Office should be challenged.

The next afternoon a headline in the *Auckland Star* was: 'Toll operator threatened with dismissal for saying Kia ora.'

Anyway, the next move came from the prime minister, Rob Muldoon, who returned from an overseas trip and said: 'I've been overseas deciding the economics of this country and I get back here and some girl wants to say Kee ora. Well, as far as I'm concerned, she can say Kee ora. Just as long as she doesn't wanna say Gidday Blue.' And that was the end of it. It was all over.

I then left tolls and went to the teachers' training college in Auckland. I was one of forty fluent Māori speakers from around the country who entered into Te Atakura and trained how to teach te reo Māori. I taught at Henderson High for three years.

After that, I went to work in health and we've

been able to make some major changes there. I think the country has moved on considerably from the 'kia ora' days. There's more acceptance now that we're all Kiwi. There are still some little pockets of people who still want to be a Pākehā. But, in the main, we're all Kiwi. So we've come a long way.

There's still work to be done, though, with te reo Māori – where you're such a strong advocate – and in politics, where you've become more and more involved. To the point where you're the president of the Māori Party.

Well, I agreed to be the president of the Māori Party to support Tariana Turia's kaupapa. It took great courage for her to cross the floor on behalf of iwi katoa. So I support her, and I support that stance. The challenge today, I think, is that we need to convince our people that it is to their benefit for their Māori Party to be sitting at the table of government.

We can disagree, and do disagree, with government. But we are sitting at the table to negotiate for the things that our people need. We get nothing in Opposition. Nothing! So, I'm happy for us to be there and to be advocating on behalf of our people.

What about retirement? And your family goals?

I'm hoping to retire at some stage. But, I don't know. Retire from what? I suppose I won't ever get to retire totally. But one goal is that my mokopuna – as many of my mokopuna as possible – can kōrero te reo. And another is that not one of them will ever go into the hands of Child, Youth and Family. Not one. And that goes for my mokopuna tuarua as well. As I mentioned earlier, I've got 22 greats under the age of ten. So it's time for me to help mould them.

LINDA TUHIWAI SMITH
TRANSFORMING EDUCATION

Professor Linda Tuhiwai Te Rina Smith now operates from Waikato University, but her influence extends well beyond New Zealand. Her work examines how, in the ongoing process of colonisation, Māori and other indigenous people have suffered and still suffer from mainstream education systems that undermine their confidence, their pride and their identity. For many years, she has been in the business of challenging and changing that. She talked with Dale Husband in July 2015.

Dale Husband: *One of the many interesting things about you is your middle name, Tuhiwai. What's the story behind that?*

Linda Tuhiwai Smith: The name Tuhiwai was given to me when I was an adult. It was a name exchange between my family and the Anderson whānau of Te Kūiti. My father is from Te Teko and is a cousin of Graham Anderson.

After the death of my grandmother Paranihia Moko, Graham Anderson's whānau came and asked my father if they could name their new mokopuna after her. My father said: 'See that young woman over there? She's always wanted a Māori name. You need to give her a name.' So they gave me the name of their grandmother, Tuhiwai.

Tuhiwai is a relation of mine, so I also whakapapa to her. Now that I work in the Waikato, I've discovered a whole lot of descendants of Tuhiwai in Kāwhia.

My maiden name was Mead because my father is Hirini Moko Mead of Ngāti Awa. And the maiden name of June, my mother, was Walker. She's Ngāti Porou from Ruatōria.

Receiving the name Tuhiwai felt good because it wasn't just a random choice. There was a relationship, a connection. I had agreed to it. And it reconnects my ties to that side of our whakapapa.

Let's go back to your growing up. Where was that? Te Teko? Ruatōria?

No. I was born in Whakatāne, but my parents were teachers, so we moved around quite a bit. My father taught in Rūātoki, and we spent many years in Waimārama in the Hawke's Bay. Next it was Whatawhata near Hamilton, and then Auckland.

I used to envy all my cousins because they went

23

to just one primary school and only one secondary school.

For secondary school, I chose Waikato Diocesan for a couple of years. But then I went to the United States when my father was doing his PhD. First, I went to high school in Illinois and then college for a wee while in Salem, Massachusetts. When I came back to Aotearoa, I did a bursary year at Auckland Girls' Grammar.

My parents didn't seem, in my view, to actively manage my education. I felt I had a lot of autonomy and freedom to choose my pathway. I remember complaining that they never came to report nights – and my mother would say: 'Why? We know what you're doing. We know what you're good at. Why would we come to listen to those teachers?'

I wonder if that American experience helped you to learn to stand on your own two feet – helped build your confidence.

I did learn to be independent and to have a good measure of myself. You may not believe this but, before I left New Zealand, I was intensely shy, reserved and quiet. I wouldn't put up my hand to ask a question. I was very respectful. I lacked confidence.

Initially, when I went from Waikato Diocesan to a co-ed school in the US, I used to stand up when a teacher entered the room. Then a teacher pulled me aside and said: 'You don't ever need to do that.

You're a learner, and you've got to stick up for yourself in this environment.'

That experience changed my trajectory, I think. So when I came back into a school setting in New Zealand, I just couldn't believe how passive New Zealand students, especially Māori students, were.

I came back to what was the seventh form and they were fussing about things that weren't of any interest to me. So I asked if I could form a politics club. I got hauled before the principal – and I was asked why I couldn't just be like everyone else and join in the other clubs.

So it's no surprise that, when I went on to Auckland University, I joined Ngā Tamatoa. In fact, I was one of the founding members. Being out in the world and having my horizons widened – and also learning that I had a mind that I could exercise – well, that was very empowering for me.

Can you tell us something about the US high school that you attended?

It was Carbondale Community High School in southern Illinois. At that time, we were really poor. So my mother made my graduation dress out of cheap curtain material – and I couldn't afford to go to the school ball or engage in a number of the social activities that American kids did.

I hung out with the poor white kids from the trailer park down the road from where we lived. And I had a couple of other mates from working-class families. Then, the day I graduated, many of the boys got their draft notices to go to Vietnam. They were recruited into the army. The rich boys went on to university and joined the National Guard and that sort of thing, so they were able to defer any service in Vietnam.

For me, it was a really interesting experience – and it gave me an understanding of, and a feel for, American education. One of the things I came to appreciate was the loyalty in the US to the military.

You could go into a lot of poor communities – American Indian and African American – and they'd always have American flags there. And that loyalty reminds me of the Māori situation here where a lot of our men have found jobs in the military and have put their lives on the line for a country that can also be quite racist to Māori.

Now, those Ngā Tamatoa days when you were a university student. How was all that?

Among my contemporaries were Taura Eruera – and Syd and Hana Jackson, who had big public profiles. Then there was Larry Parr and Pauline Kingi too, Josie Keelan in Wellington, Orewa Barrett Ohia in Te Awamutu. We also had people like Pat Hohepa and Rangi Walker who would support some of our activities.

It was an interesting group. But there were difficult times and occasionally we were spat on by Māori people who thought we were being outrageous. We'd be told that we were being disrespectful, that it wasn't our place to be protesting, and that we were disturbing the peace.

But I think there's a tendency to romanticise that era of early activism in the 1970s. People may think Ngā Tamatoa had a cast of thousands, but actually it was a very small organisation. People came in and out. But it was still able to voice particular concerns and to articulate them in a way that caught attention – and it was able to mobilise Māori.

At that time, there were other things going on. The gay and lesbian movement. Feminist movement. Anti-war movement. Anti-racist movement.

But in Ngā Tamatoa we were staunch because we thought this was a Māori movement and we needed to keep that grounded in who we were, our identity, our whenua, our history and our rights. So one of our messages was about the Treaty of Waitangi and another was about te reo.

I suppose that this period of Māori revitalisation gave an impetus to the academic journey that you're still on, with a focus on indigenous concepts, and on what First Nations people can offer the global community.

Yes. Absolutely. I think it gave me a drive that made me engage in academic studies with a purpose. I wasn't just rolling along to university thinking:

'Oh well, I'll end up being a teacher of history.' I was looking for particular kinds of knowledge.

When I couldn't find it in the university, I'd read more radical texts. Malcolm X for example. Or Frantz Fanon. They helped radicalise my mind. But, more than that – it gave me a purpose and showed me why education is important.

One of my roles in Ngā Tamatoa was to go and talk to hostile audiences, mostly in secondary schools, but also in the communities, about why the Treaty was important. And, really, that's where I cut my teeth as a communicator. I had to stand up and learn how to give a message. Not get all emotionally tied up in it. Try not to cry when they said mean things about Māori people and racist things about us.

I had to learn not only how you can give a message, and provide information that's factually correct, but also how you tell the Māori story in a way that people get what we were about. We didn't think we were radical. We just thought we were asserting what was our right and what had been promised to us.

So to get a backlash, which is still happening in New Zealand, wasn't surprising, but it was so venomous, so hostile and so aggressive.

Ngā Tamatoa was actually a pacifist group. We did protests. We did lots of speeches. We did petitions. We would show up at events and put up placards. But we didn't believe in violence. We believed in communicating.

And yet people could be very violent to us.

We often did things where the men had to stand in front of us because people were so hostile. And it wasn't just Pākehā people. There were lots of Māori who were hostile as well.

Those Ngā Tamatoa days, it seems, must have strengthened your belief that education is the way forward for Māori.

Yes. I see education as THE platform for the future for us. Education, to me, sets individuals free. It gives individuals choices. And, because I believe that, I see education as an important fight. And we have to make sure that it works for us because, for a hundred and something years, schools haven't worked for us. Nor have the universities.

I see my current role as changing the way our institutions work with Māori. Transforming those institutions. Transforming the curriculum. Ensuring that, when Māori come to university, they don't have to leave their Māori identity at the door. Or they don't have to put a hard shell around that identity to protect it – so they can engage successfully as Māori.

The role of education institutions is to harness that identity, give it a bit of discipline, but develop it rather than crush it. When they crush our spirits, as they still do for many of our young people, that's what keeps me engaged in the struggle to transform these places.

As an academic, you've been doing research, lecturing here and overseas – and you've been writing too about the impact of colonisation on us and other indigenous people. I understand that you feel it's essential for Māori to know our own story.

I think it's really important that we should all know the barriers, the struggles, the achievements and triumphs of our tīpuna in coping with colonisation. It's really important to know why we're in the predicament we're in and to know that there's a backstory which is full of history that we were not taught in schools. Full of particular histories of our people as iwi, hapū and as whānau.

I think a significant part of decolonisation is knowing our story and rediscovering ourselves. Not just saying we are a proud people because we can do kapa haka and perform, but knowing fundamentally that we are a proud and accomplished people who navigated the Pacific, who designed technologies, who created great systems and who valued knowledge. And that's where we come from.

Those are the platforms that take us forward. And our people need to know that. Not in an arrogant way. But knowing it deeply so that we can say: 'This is what gives me a place here. This means I can achieve.'

KENNEDY WARNE
AN AWAKENING FOR A PĀKEHĀ

Kennedy Warne is the founding editor, and now editor-at-large, of New Zealand Geographic. *He is also the author of* Tūhoe: Portrait of a Nation. *This piece was published in March 2016.*

Though it was more than a quarter of a century ago, I still remember the day I began to wake up.

It was 1989. *New Zealand Geographic*, the magazine I co-founded and edited with the publisher, John Woods, was less than a year old. One of our photographers, Arno Gasteiger, had produced a set of evocative images of the Spirits Bay–Cape Rēinga area, and I was keen to publish them.

I had pictures, but no text. Who could write words that would catch the essence of that spiritually charged landscape – the leaping place of the departed?

Arno had a name: Saana Murray. She was a poet, an elder of Ngāti Kurī, the tribe of that place, and a keeper of the long-burning fires of her people.

After some phoning around, I found that she was in Ōtara, staying with the family of one of her thirteen children. I drove to the house and showed her the photographs and asked if she would be willing to write something. What she wrote was up to her, I said. I wanted the words to support, but not explain, the pictures. Above all, I wanted to capture the spirit.

Saana agreed. Then, nervously and apologetically – deadlines were looming; deadlines were *always* looming – I asked how soon she could deliver the text. What she told me I have never forgotten. 'I cannot write anything here,' she said. 'I will have to go to the land.'

She said it as if she were stating the obvious. Yet it was the first time I had heard such a thing: that words about the land required the presence of the land. That knowledge was inseparable from its context.

For someone steeped in scientific thinking – a mindset in which knowledge is a commodity, endlessly transferable – it was a challenging thought. For a moment, the fabric of my fact-based worldview started to fray, and I caught a glimpse of another country.

I've come to learn that this is the country Māori

inhabit. In the Māori worldview, context is vital. Knowledge is not disembodied information but part of a living matrix of encounters and relationships, past and present, natural and spiritual.

Saana cared deeply about Māori knowledge, and she asserted that the tangata whenua are its rightful and necessary custodians. She believed that the Treaty of Waitangi guaranteed the custodianship of Māori things by Māori people, and it pained her that that guarantee had not been honoured. Yet Saana never stopped believing in the Treaty. 'I was born to the tune of the Tiriti of Waitangi,' she wrote. It was a tune she would sing all her life.

A SPIRIT'S FLIGHT

Two years after we published the Spirits Bay story, Saana and five other iwi representatives lodged the Wai 262 'flora and fauna' claim with the Waitangi Tribunal. It was a claim, among other things, about Māori control of Māori intellectual property. When, after twenty years of research and deliberation, the tribunal delivered its report in 2011, Saana was the only one of the original claimants still alive to read it.

Then, later that year, she passed, too.

I heard the news while driving to the Bay of Islands. It was already the last day of the tangi, and she was to be buried that afternoon at Spirits Bay. There was little chance I would get there in time, but I wanted to pay my respects to a woman whose influence I had felt for twenty years. So I kept driving.

It was dark when I arrived at te muri o te motu. As I'd expected, the tangi was over. The place seemed deserted. Then I heard dance music and children's laughter and the clink of bottles coming from a small marquee surrounded by a clutch of cars and caravans. I walked over.

'I'm looking for the whānau of Saana Murray,' I said.

'You've found it. Come and join us for a beer.'

I sat in the tent with a smoked trevally and a Lion Red and listened as one of the granddaughters-in-law told me about Saana's passing. Saana had felt, at long last, that her work for the iwi was done. She had fought her battles and could rest now. So when the latest bout of illness came, she let herself be taken. Hers was a completed life. How many of the living achieve such closure at death?

I knew about a few of her battles. When her own mother lay dying, she had asked Saana to promise that she would endeavour to 'retrieve the land and ratify the Treaty'. Land and Treaty became the wellsprings of Saana's energy and passion. For forty years she pleaded her people's cause to politicians, ombudsmen, governor-generals, talkshow hosts, judges, even the secretary-general of the United Nations.

She once joked that she'd go down in history as 'the Great Objector'. She objected to the Europeanisation of her people. She objected to Pākehā trampling of the Treaty. She objected to 'laws with claws like parasites, devouring my human rights'.

One of her battles was over sand – specifically the dazzling white sands at the entrance to Pārengarenga Harbour, the raw material of New Zealand glass manufacture. The dunes were Ngāti Kurī land. A century of mining and dredging had left the dunes scarred, vegetation damaged and kai moana smothered. Saana fought to stop her people's land being sucked away for Pākehā profit. She prevailed, and today the dunes lie unmolested, glittering in the sun.

'She's buried on the hill over there,' one of the whānau told me. 'You can go up if you want.'

In the dark, I followed the path that led to a tiny urupā. Just four graves. It was a path Saana would have walked often, for her own son is buried there. Saana's plot was mounded up with sand and covered with flowers, kete and keepsakes. Jammed into the middle of it was a young tī kōuka. Its long leaves were rattling in the wind – a quiet anthem of the north.

The moon was up and the surf was glowing in its light. The scene was uncannily similar to the opening photograph of our Spirits Bay story, two decades earlier, in which a solitary white bird soars across a wide expanse of sea. I had entitled the story 'A spirit's flight'. Those words sat well in my mind as I bade farewell to another spirit, flying away home.

A FORECOURT MARAE

On my way back south that night, something happened that, in its way, was as emphatic as anything I learned from Saana. It was another small awakening from the long sleep of Pākehā-centric thought.

I was driving the coast road through Doubtless Bay, and my fuel gauge was way past empty. In my haste to get to the tangi, I hadn't filled up, expecting that there'd be at least one petrol station in the Far North open at night. Fat chance. By the time I got to Kaeo, I knew I wasn't going to make it much further. No worries, I thought. I'll find a rest area and sleep under the Hilux till morning.

Then I spotted a truck stop with a card reader. I drove in to see if the antiquated machine would recognise my credit card. It clicked and whirred and spat my card back out. Transaction error. I tried two or three more times, then gave up.

I was about to drive off to look for a spot to sleep when a fish delivery truck pulled in. The driver had a fuel card that would work in the machine, and I asked if he would mind putting $30 of diesel in my vehicle after he'd filled his, and I'd give him cash for it.

He nodded and, while he was filling up, I started telling him why I was in the north and the history I'd had with Saana and why I didn't want to let the opportunity pass by. He didn't say much, just listened while the Pākehā said what was on his mind.

He hung up the nozzle and I held out my hand with the bills. He looked at me and said: 'Put your money away.'

That's all he said, but I felt as if I'd been jolted by a live wire. It was another glimpse into the Māori world, another wake-up call. There are times when money has no place and no importance. At that fuel stop in Kaeo, two strangers were holding their own tangi. That forecourt was our marae.

SOUL OF THE FOREST

A year later I was in Te Urewera, writing about Tūhoe's long walk towards justice and having a little more cultural sleep rubbed out of my eyes.

One night, at Clifford and Kuini Akuhata's house at Waimana, some whānau were explaining the meaning of matemateaone. It was a feeling of being wrapped and cocooned by the earth, one of them said. Like being privy to the yearning that Ranginui, the sky father, feels for Papatūānuku, the earth mother from whom he is eternally separated.

'It's like being in a spell,' she said. 'Sometimes when I'm walking in the forest I get the taste of Papatūānuku on my palate. There's a sudden sense of sweetness. "Hmmm," you think. "What's that?" It's no particular flower or plant. It's just the taste of health. Other times, at night, the sky can feel like an ocean of stars and you seem to have stepped off the edge of the earth. You're dizzy, but you don't want the experience to stop. It's too special.'

I had felt those very things in the Urewera forests. Once, at midnight, I stepped outside a hut on a high ridge and almost stumbled with vertigo. The stars were thicker than I'd ever seen – great clusters of light spangling the sky – while immense trees thrust upwards to greet them.

At dawn, I walked to a bluff with a view of mist-wreathed valleys and listened to kōkako, the soul of the forest, the bird that Tūhoe say mediates between wairua time and people time. Kōkako seem not to simply sing their notes, but send them into the world as gifts, painting the forest with song, drawing the listener into the music.

In such times, the curtain between natural and supernatural feels thin, like a membrane allowing passage from one side to the other. The more I get to know te ao Māori, the thinner that membrane seems to get.

It's an idea that sits awkwardly in the Western worldview, but comfortably in the Māori one.

Physical and spiritual are children of the same parents. Intimations from beyond are known, expected and trusted – though less so today than in the past, when Pākehā thinking had yet to erode Māori cosmology. Te Kooti, whose presence is often felt in the hills of Te Urewera, was one who 'lived by the omens of the sky, thunder and the rainbow, and waited for the time that they told', wrote Judith Binney, one of our historians.

I had an inkling of that, coming back from possum trapping with Maynard Apiata and two of his sons, up the Whakatāne river. As we walked our horses across shallow streams, the iron of the horseshoes ringing on the smooth river stones, I was sure I heard a babble of voices behind me. I looked over my shoulder several times, scanning the steep bluffs that rose on all sides, but saw no one. But the sounds seemed unmistakeable, and I wondered what battles might have been fought here, and who had travelled these river roads generations before, and what ghost band of hunters or hunted was making its presence known.

Tūhoe take this sort of experience in their stride, incorporating it into a life narrative that interweaves many ways of knowing.

And, really, this is what Saana Murray showed me all those years ago, when she said she had to go to the place where the knowledge belongs.

I'm pushing sixty. It's taken me most of my life to wake up and start to learn what Saana was on about. But hers is a catchy tune, and it's the one I want to sing.

MOANA MANIAPOTO
TANGIHANGA – A DYING TRADITION

Moana Maniapoto (Te Arawa, Ngāti Tūwharetoa) is a musician – she was inducted into the New Zealand Music Hall of Fame in 2016 – documentary maker, te reo advocate, political activist and columnist. This piece was published in August 2015.

As a child, I remember seeing our mother dressed entirely in black, wearing a hat, veil and sombre expression. I asked where she was going.

'A funeral,' she said.

'Can I come?' I asked.

'No,' she replied. 'Kids don't go to funerals.'

Granddad lived in Christchurch. We lived in Invercargill. He may as well have lived on another planet, geographically and culturally. Mum, a Pākehā, told us about the first tangi she ever went to. Dad's whānau hosted relatives at home in Rotorua.

'People were everywhere, sleeping on the floor and constantly eating,' she recalled. 'We seemed to be forever washing dishes.'

Mum is now so used to tangi that she finds funerals strange. 'How odd,' she'll whisper, if there's no singing or speeches at the graveside.

Tangihanga is the ultimate Māori cultural expression, the most resilient of our traditions. Full of ritual and emotion, tangi are a showcase of oratory, song and storytelling.

'It's theatre, like a live play,' says Selwyn Parata, a Ngāti Porou leader. 'Kuia wailing, karanga, mōteatea and oriori – these all set the ambience.'

It's the space where relationships are celebrated, challenged and nurtured. It's where talk turns to politics, sports, business and gossip. Tangihanga is probably *the* most powerful networking event in te ao Māori. Emotion is encouraged and drama is expected. It's a time to balance the ledger of kinship responsibility.

And, at its heart, is whanaungatanga and manaakitanga.

Potty-mouthed Gordon Ramsay, the TV chef, would be lost for words if he saw marae cooks in action, catering for hundreds, sometimes thousands, for three, four or five days on very little sleep. No sweat for them to whip out a song either.

When it comes to tangihanga, it's all hands on deck. The mana of the marae is at stake. Tangi are talked about for years after. Stories of coffins spirited away in stealth, full-blown concerts, high drama and shared memories.

I can still see my Uncle Hitiri slowly rise in the pouring rain to farewell my former father-in-law, Bob Jackson, as he lay at Te Puea in Māngere. Bending against the elements, the act of shrugging off his heavy coat seemed such a noble and respectful gesture.

Who can forget the five-hour wait in atrocious storms at the tangi of the three Stirling brothers? No one complained.

'Now we have to adjust tikanga because younger generations don't want to get wet,' says Selwyn Parata. 'And you want them to come to marae.'

I remember the spectacular haka face-off at the tangi of our Ngāti Tūwharetoa ariki Hepi Te Heuheu, where a vortex of wairua seemed to engulf the performers. It wrapped itself around Tumu Te Heuheu as well, as he stepped into the dark ancestral vault. Alone.

Māori funerals can be hilarious. As the relatives and friends of Maui Prime cracked hysterical jokes at his expense, I half expected Dalvanius to leap out of his coffin and yell: 'How dare you?' And then to burst into giggles himself.

What about the time a calf trotted on to the marae behind an unsuspecting Temuera Morrison as he paid tribute to Wi Kuki Kaa? Parekura

Horomia took off his coat and morphed into a nimble-footed matador.

Sitting beside the coffin is often the best seat in town. One mischievous aunt would give us the giggles with her running commentary on the 'city cousins' as they moved tentatively on to the marae. 'Aue! Look at those two,' she'd say. 'Going the wrong way. No idea.'

Selwyn Parata says the role of kuia was to 'provide the ambience'.

'We don't know how to cry any more. Those old kuia could switch the waterworks on and off no trouble. They'd think of those who passed, those left behind and, because kuia were also fasting, it wasn't hard to wail. Nowadays some whānau struggle to sing or even share stories.'

It used to be that on the final night, the singing and storytelling lasted until daybreak. That's how it was at the tangi of Ngoi Pewhairangi, Selwyn said, because no one wanted to sleep. 'They loved being together.'

I remember the late Marj Rau-Kupa wailing when the wharenui lights were switched off at 9 p.m. 'What's wrong with you people? You have to sing *all night long*!'

At 5 a.m., she threw the switch and ordered everyone up, helpfully rolling stunned children out of their slumber by pulling their blankets out from under them. She insisted manuhiri would arrive 'any minute now'. By 6 a.m., fed, watered and poised like coiled springs, we peered into the dawn. Not a visitor in sight.

Hone Edwards counts the recent tangi of Anzac Pikia as very special.

'It was like Matatini,' says Hone. 'Everyone knew Anzac's passion was haka, so Iti Kahurangi, Waka Huia, Te Arawa all turned up to perform on the last night.'

Back in the day, you never took photographs at tangi. Nowadays, tangihanga are not only filmed, but some are livestreamed. Hone remembers when, as a *Te Karere* reporter in 1983, he approached one whānau to film for the very first time.

'A respected matakite, I believed her passing would interest the motu because this kuia helped hundreds,' said Hone. 'The whānau were dubious but eventually allowed cameras half way up the marae ātea. No filming the atamira, coffin, or photographs.'

The passing of Te Arikinui Te Atairangikaahu broke new ground. Understanding that Te Arikinui was near death, Hone gained permission from Tainui and his television board, then approached whānau pani, the bereaved family.

'They didn't want to discuss it,' he recalls. '*He karanga mate*. They said I was pre-empting her death. I said it was going to happen and there would be chaos if they opened the marae up to untold cameras. I had a budget, two outside broadcasting trucks, five cameras, and a commitment to share footage with any broadcaster. That was a first.'

At 2 a.m. on the morning of her death, the whānau contacted Hone. Te Arikinui's tangi was filmed daily, a highlights package broadcast each night, and the actual burial day went live to air.

The tangi of Erima Henare, Parekura Horomia and Api Mahuika have since been livestreamed.

Naida Glavish isn't opposed to filming. She says it helps those absent with the grieving process. She says koha is something else that's changed. Selwyn agrees: 'Some have a romantic idea about marae – that marae pay for everything.'

Naida says some marae are forced to set fees because koha are so unreliable. Those who can't afford traditional tangi take their deceased home. Or stay at the funeral parlour until burial day.

It's not just about cost either.

'Some aren't on the Māori map, so they're whakamā,' says Hone. 'They take their tangi into their houses where they can relax and express their warmth naturally. Sometimes they share memories around a BBQ. Even a few of my Pākehā mates have taken their funerals into their homes.'

Then there's cremation. Selwyn says they've occasionally placed an urn on the whāriki. Finding out that Peter Buck was cremated (because he died overseas) helped Selwyn adjust his thinking. Patu

Hohepa thinks cost is a factor because his whānau were quoted $30,000 to fly a body from Australia to New Zealand. He said cremation was carried out during the Musket Wars and that some ashes and *heads* were brought home.

Can't quite see that catching on.

Then there's the dress code. In the old days, mourners would wear their Sunday best. Recently, I've seen both sexes rock up in Swannies, shorts and trackies. I've yet to see a man in a frock though.

'When you pass over, our people describe it as the beginning of the journey beyond the hidden veil … *ki tua o te ārai,*' says Hone. 'I've always thought the veil is a perfect metaphor for men in drag also, because it hides all sorts of secrets. Your manliness for one.'

Twenty years after his cousin Witoria (Pussy Galore) Drake died, Hone recalls a clash of two cultures at the tangi: te ao Māori and the explosive, flamboyant drag queens of K Road. It kept him busy.

'Kaumātua couldn't cope with men running around the marae in dresses with falsetto voices,' he said. 'They couldn't get their heads around it.'

Kaumātua instructed Hone that men *cannot* wear dresses at tangihanga. 'Shite,' said Hone. 'These were queens, not men. Or men who were queens. Whatever, it wasn't the way my elders saw it. What lay behind the hidden veil was uncertainty, verging on prejudice and intolerance.'

The stroppy queens adjusted their wardrobe and emerged wearing ... lavalava. 'My elders were a tad confused. They couldn't cope with men in drag, but could cope with men in lavalava, even though lavalava look like dresses,' says Hone. 'Some perceptions around our customs do my head in.'

Selwyn (Ngāti Porou) and Patu (Ngāpuhi) report that customs remain pretty much the same at their rural marae. Selwyn believes tangi and marae are the base of Māori culture because they're about whanaungatanga.

As kids, in the South Island, Amiria Reriti and her brothers loved tangi. It meant fun times with the cuzzies. 'At Rāpaki, we'd play hide and seek. At night, we'd be around the fire cooking spuds in foil. Tuahiwi was different ... too many bossy, grumpy types there. You were on edge in case you got stuck with some ugly job.'

While I had a relatively late start, my kids have attended tangi since they were babies. They're used to tangihanga. They know what's going on and how to behave. They've seen dead bodies. They can handle the emotion.

After all, Māori believe the more wailing and carrying-on, the better. It's healthy. It honours the dead. And makes it easy to explain death.

'So Aunty won't drive her car any more?' asked my son, a concerned four-year-old peering into an open casket. 'She won't go to McDonald's again?'

The tangi is important because it helps adults to prepare children for the inevitable loss of their grandparents and parents. And to accept that death is part of life and that life will go on without us in it.

While some ritual may be tweaked, it remains the most authentic of all Māori cultural practices. It is the absolute manifestation of Māori beliefs and an acknowledgement of constant communion between the spiritual and human worlds. If we cease to celebrate life and death in the way of our ancestors, our very existence as Māori will be under threat.

But, for now, the tangihanga – our dying tradition – is very much alive.

ELIOTA FUIMAONO-SAPOLU
SAD DAYS AT AUCKLAND GRAMMAR

Eliota Fuimaono-Sapolu had an outstanding career as a rugby player for more than twenty years – as a Manurewa junior; then in the first XV for Auckland Grammar; in 23 test matches for Manu Samoa (including the 2007 and 2011 World Cups); as a professional in the United Kingdom for Bath (43 games) and Gloucester (54); and in Japan for the Coca-Cola West Red Sparks. But he has also made headlines as an uncompromising critic of the racism in and beyond the rugby establishment. He talked to Dale in November 2015, just after the Rugby World Cup.

Dale Husband: *Kia ora, Eliota. I understand that you were born in Samoa, that you came to New Zealand as a three-year-old, that your family eventually settled in Manurewa – and that you spent your high school*

years at Auckland Grammar, which probably was
fairly white in those days.

Eliota Fuimaono-Sapolu: My schools in
Manurewa were predominantly Māori and Pacific,
so I had no idea what Auckland Grammar would
be like. But the school was completely different
from Manurewa where I was raised. I felt very
comfortable around Polynesian and Māori people
and then I was off to a school where there were
about five of us.

There were (and there are) white supremacy
attitudes right through the school system. I
remember this general knowledge question in
primary school: *Who discovered New Zealand?* And
I wrote: *Māori discovered New Zealand.* And that
was wrong. I was told the correct answer was Abel
Tasman. Even though there were Māori people
already here in New Zealand, it was very important
for us to learn that a white person was 'first'.

That was at primary school. And then you go
to Auckland Grammar where it's complete white
supremacy, and you concentrate on white history
no matter how irrelevant. Try finding a practical
situation where knowing all the British kings and
queens is relevant. See if you need that anywhere in
life. But that's what I learned at Auckland Grammar.

Then, after five years there, I go to university
and they ask us about the Treaty of Waitangi. And
I'm like: 'What the hell is this?' I knew nothing

about Māori. I knew everything British. I knew everything white. I knew nothing about the Pacific. I learned nothing about Māori. Nothing at that school.

We're taught a lot of lies at school. A lot of rubbish. We're not taught a lot of truth. I look back now – it's just so bad. We learn about Captain Cook, but we don't learn about his Polynesian navigator, Tupaia, who showed him where to go. Cook even writes about Tupaia who was telling them, for instance, to stay away from that island because there's a reef right there, or to call in on this island because it has more supplies.

Cook has this Polynesian navigator right there with him in his very first voyage, and he's spelling that out in his diary. But there's nothing about Tupaia in the New Zealand school curriculum. Instead, there's all this irrelevant stuff about the English kings and queens – and, if you don't learn that, you don't pass. They force us to learn it. And yet it has no use. Absolutely no practical use.

And, while they're putting these things in our education system, they're taking away our own identity and our own belief in ourselves and our culture. It's a process of colonising our minds – and so we have to try and decolonise our minds and un-learn these things in the hope that we can help our next generation to develop their own self-belief.

This sounds like kōrero from Ngā Tamatoa or

the Polynesian Panthers. And I respect that, because our young people do need to gauge the value and the relevance of what they're being taught. But I suppose, when you raised any of these issues, it would've put you offside.

It always got me offside. At Auckland Grammar, I was constantly in trouble, always on detention. I stood up in history class and asked: 'Why are we learning everything white, and there's nothing brown here?' I was at the stage where I was questioning everything and I really didn't care what the reaction might be.

Outside the classroom it was different because I won the best all-rounder award in the first XV. There were some big names who'd won it in earlier years. Like Grant Fox and Martin Crowe. But I could never be a prefect. When you challenge their white world, if they perceive a threat, you're pushed to the side.

What's your attitude now that you look back on your years at what some would consider the most prestigious school in New Zealand? Do you resent going there?

I was very lucky that I had a mother who doesn't have anything like the conventional view of the world. I notice that a number of Polynesian guys from that school are very confident. I don't think they're confident in themselves being Polynesian. They're confident with that sense of entitlement, that: 'I went to Auckland Grammar. I can say what I want.' Their confidence comes from that privileged schooling.

I don't know. Maybe people want to keep on sending their children there, but I think it's important that we find ways to empower the schools which are predominantly Māori and Polynesian. And that we give these kids the knowledge to decolonise, and to find the brilliance in themselves – so they know their history and their achievers and the beautiful, genius things they should be celebrating within our cultures.

I tautoko what you're saying. But, despite the prejudices of the education system, Māori and Polynesian emancipation has been proceeding. You're an example of that. And perhaps, in a way, your experiences at Auckland Grammar have helped you formulate your ideas.

Yes, definitely, because I was always on this quest. But another element is something in our history. Why is my mother so brilliant? She's fresh. She can barely speak English properly and yet she's a genius. She's fearless. Everywhere we'd go, if we weren't treated right, she'd just say it.

There's been this narrative from our colonisers that we are savages. Many Pālagi and Pākehā embrace the narrative that we're savages. And that helps justify and perpetuate the racism in our society.

You've just mentioned your mum. Could we take a moment to touch on your parents' background?

Well, Mum and Dad came over with us from Samoa in the early 1980s. My mother was from Vaiala and Fagaloa, and my father from Falelatai. He came here to study medicine. In the beginning, we were living in a one-bedroom flat in Grafton – and then in Grey Lynn. But once my mother graduated and became a lawyer we moved south to Manurewa. As kids we spent quite a bit of time in her law office, and law was pretty much all I wanted as a career. In our law firm, we haven't specialised. So we do everything – family, criminal, conveyancing, the lot.

Let's turn back now to your concern about the mindset that encourages a disparaging view of Polynesians.

Well, it is an important issue. And I've done a DVD to try to counter that attitude. It's called: *This is the Pacific history that they don't teach at school.* I worked on that as a result of attending schools which don't teach that Pacific history. Which don't teach our children about the genocide in West Papua. Or about the efforts to exterminate Aboriginals in Australia. Or about what happened to Māori in New Zealand.

I made the DVD because of my experiences in these white supremacist schools that taught nothing about us when they could have been telling us about Tupaia, and how Polynesians invented surfing, and about our brilliant ancient navigators, and about any number of other Polynesian achievements.

James Cook recognised the talent and the achievements. He wrote that the Polynesians were the most extraordinary race he'd ever come across. Here we were navigating the oceans. This brown race was unbelievable. But that doesn't get any attention in the history our kids are taught because, well, God forbid, those brown people might be perceived as superior to the white ones.

So that's why I made the DVD.

Unfortunately, this type of kōrero coming from you, a young Samoan man, is not the norm. Our own people, especially the older generation, are conservative and, as colonised people, many have become compliant. So I suspect that, when you're challenging their style and their viewpoints, you're getting offside with them.

Oh, absolutely. Especially at home. In Samoa, in order to run for parliament, you have to have a matai title. You have to have a cultural matai title bestowed on you. Yet, in Samoa, over half the villages don't offer a matai title to women. So, for me, I don't care if I'm offside. These are real issues that we need to address. But the great thing about it is that a lot of youth are raising questions. And I'm encouraging the questions by directing the DVD at youth. It's in six-minute clips because youth want their information quick.

Old people are a bit harder to change and are stuck in their ways, which is fine and I don't condemn them. We're here by virtue of our elders. Because of them, we have survived. Thankfully. The most important thing for our ancestors who were facing extermination was survive. Just survive.

Then there'll be a generation who will bring us back. Who will bring us back to who we *really* are. Bring back our female leaders. Bring back our culture – everything. This world needs who we really are. You look at climate change, the pollution, the over-population, the corporatisation. This world is self-destructing simply because we've gone away from indigenous principles.

I'm intrigued by our Māori and Pasifika relationships. At one time in my life, I thought we were distinct peoples. But, as I've got older, I've come to feel that our whakapapa connections are real. That we are cousins. That we are whānau. Is that how you see us now?

Absolutely. And we need to accept that as well. Politically, the European colonisers were brilliant with their 'divide and conquer'. They divided the Pacific people into these little islands by destroying our boats. They went around the islands using their cannons and destroyed every single double-hulled vessel they saw. They conceded that these Pacific boats were bigger and faster. So they destroyed them to limit our people to their islands.

And that's why no one navigates now, even though there are still Tongan elders who talk about the voyages that the Tongans made to New Zealand to hunt the moa. And in the Cook Islands and Tahiti, for instance, there are stories of their navigators and their voyages, including journeys to New Zealand.

But the links are everywhere in our languages. Like in *alofa, aroha* or *aloha.* In our numbers too: *tasi, lua, tolu, fa* and *tahi, rua, toru, whā.* And in the legend of Māui who wasn't just the discoverer of Aotearoa but also of Tonga and Hawai'i. It's all there. But, unfortunately, the colonisers did this brilliant number on us, just as they did in Africa. They knew how to colonise the mind – and the people. You have to divide people. Which is what they did with us. They divided and conquered. So now we need to take back who we were and who we are. But at the same time, I can definitely see that this is the land of the Māori. This is Aotearoa.

That kind of kōrero inevitably ruffles the feathers of the establishment. And you've done the same with your criticisms of the self-serving nature of the rugby establishment here and overseas. You haven't been impressed by the rugby bosses' habit of short-changing the Pacific Island countries – and for taking almost forever to organise an All Black trip for a test match in Samoa.

Yeah, the attitude has been bad enough in New Zealand with its history of kowtowing to South Africa and leaving Māori players out of the All Black teams touring South Africa because the South Africans didn't want brown-skinned players visiting them. At least the NZRFU eventually apologised for that.

But for us Samoans, it's worse. At least when the All Blacks tour England, and you sell out Twickenham, there's a fixed fee of like two million pounds, that goes straight to the All Blacks. But when Samoa plays England, and it's a sell-out at Twickenham, Samoa gets nothing. England will get seven million pounds, just like that, and Samoa gets nothing.

So we're always having to fight. We're contributing so much to world rugby and getting back so little. Take the World Cup games in the last month or so. All four of the Manu Samoa games were sold out and the IRB – the International Rugby Board – is going to pay Samoa 150,000 pounds. That's 10,000 pounds *less* than Samoa TV had to pay for the rights to show our games to Samoa.

Meanwhile, in Ward 5 of our hospital in Apia, there are five young players paralysed from rugby. We get nothing to help them. There are issues like that where we have to fight. It's like trying to fight colonialism all over again. Neo-colonialism. Because we're being treated like crap.

And, when we were trying to bring the All Blacks to Samoa, it was about trying to bring some money to Samoa, to bring the tourists, to find ways of helping our economy and our rugby because we don't get anything when we tour in the UK.

So that's why our Samoan rugby is struggling. And there's another problem, which could mean rugby is dying in Samoa. American football is taking away some of our best talent. Last year they came in and now thirty of our biggest players – some of them only sixteen-year-olds – are off to colleges in the States. And for us, in Samoa, we're actually happy that kids are now not playing rugby, because the game isn't good for us.

Eliota, we appreciate your sobering comments. And when we hear you, still a young man in your thirties, taking up these issues, we can have some confidence that there are significant efforts for change. But perhaps too many of our rangatahi are politically apathetic.

No, I don't think they're apathetic. And this generation is in a much stronger position than we were. Every kid has a cellphone and that's like a super-computer in their pocket. We tend to tell them that that's the problem. But I think it's the solution because they have access to a vast array of information and perspectives and opinions.

They're in a position now where they don't have to accept the American line that they were the good guys in the Vietnam War. Or the British line about dealing with the Māori savages. They can google Vietnamese views. And Māori perspectives. They're a generation who have a chance to open up their minds.

You've had so much success in rugby that you might easily have kept your head down and not complicated your life by speaking out so forthrightly on various issues. Is that at least partly because you see high-profile personalities as having a responsibility to speak up?

I think it's very important that we don't become absorbed in our fame – partly because that fame is fleeting. But we also need to be conscious of the political issues that are affecting other players and the fans. I think we have a duty to be vocal about the policies that affect the people who watch us. There are questions about employment, taxes and affordable housing. And, as prominent sporting personalities, we're in a position to have some influence.

You're confident that we can make a better Aotearoa and a better Pacific?

Absolutely. I see so much brilliance in our Māori and Polynesian children. They're so good at so many things. Sport. Academics. Whatever. And we just have to help them believe in themselves. It's my belief in our children, our next generation, that inspires me.

SIMA URALE
THEY KNEW I WAS NAUGHTY

Sima Urale is an actor, writer, director and maker of films, documentaries, commercials and videos. For years she has gathered awards both in New Zealand and overseas, against much international competition – starting with her first film, O Tamaiti (The Children), which won the Silver Lion for Best Short Film at the Venice Film Festival in 1996. This kōrero with Dale was in November 2015.

Dale Husband: *Tēnā koe, Sima. Now, right at the start, I better make sure that I'm pronouncing your surname correctly. I suppose that Urale is pronounced* oo-rah-le.

Sima Urale: That's it. But the funny thing about that name is that, in Samoan, we don't have an R. We have an L instead. And originally the name was Ulale. But then, when Mum and Dad got married, an uncle, who married them, misspelled their name. He put an R in there. And all the paperwork went through like that. So we got stuck with this very unusual name. And our line of the family is the only one with that R.

The story of Aotearoa is largely a story of parents heading this way so as to give their kids a better shot. I understand that, in your case, it was your mother who was keen to set out from Samoa.

Yeah. The village was far too small for Mum. She's just too big for a village. She's too big for an island. In fact, she's really too big for here too. She is Pusi Urale and she's from Matavai in Savai'i. And my dad, Fatu, comes from the Gafo'i clan in Fagamalo. That's in Savai'i as well. They were two beautiful villages that we grew up in.

We were born there in grass huts. I think there was only one Western house in the whole village – and just the school buildings. But, basically, everything else was traditional fale, all made with the traditional niu. The poles, the roofs and everything.

That's all still really vivid in my mind. We'd swim with the turtles. There was no electricity so we'd cook on the fire. And all the food was fresh. You had to go and fish for your food – or into the plantations.

And, of course, you're not feeding one little nuclear family. You're feeding families of like fifty or sixty. Just like on a marae. Big extended families. And that's still the case today.

Those memories are fresh because we still go back home. We're still close to our relatives and the village life. We love it and, of course, when we take the grandkids back, and the nieces and the nephews, they're told to get out the back and do the work. You know, with our lot, you're only a guest for one day and then you better go wash the dishes.

So we make sure they go off into the plantations, and do the chores. Help out with the whānau. We all dig in. We're actually a part of it. We take care of one another.

Now, back to your mum for a moment.

She's amazing. She's broad-minded. Very liberal. Always forward-thinking. Wanting to see the world. People sometimes make the mistake of thinking that, just because we're traditional in a number of ways, we don't want to look outside the box. Well, she was very curious about foreigners. She wanted to know what was happening in the world – and she wanted us kids to see the world and not just be stuck in a plantation, even though she loved and respected our traditions and culture.

So I have to give her a lot of credit for thinking outside the box and bringing the whānau over here. It was a massive sacrifice though. Massive sacrifice, because Dad was the opposite. Dad was very rooted in the Samoan ways. But he sacrificed the lifestyle he was used to back in the islands to do what Mum wanted – and to do so for the sake of us kids. His was a huge sacrifice. And we used to cry because we knew he was sad being here.

He had to go and work in the factories. Shoe factory. Carpet factories. To support the whānau and to see the dream through, whatever that dream was. He supported us all the way. But he was really an island man.

Mum wasn't. She was just a complete opposite. Totally in love, but they were complete opposites. So it was amazing for us to grow up with parents who had such opposing views. You know, one would say: 'Don't hit.' And the other one would say: 'Hit them in the head.' All types of things. It was fascinating.

Have you thought much about why she was such a free spirit? Māori and Pasifika people have grown up hearing the myths and legends about Māui and his mischief and trickery. Do you think there was something of Māui in her?

Yeah. But that Māui spirit is in all of us, isn't it? The mischief – and the urge to explore and discover. I love the Māui legends because I think they actually do capture the naughty, cheeky aspect of our culture. Hercules, and heroes from other cultures, didn't behave the way Māui did. It's his spirit that helps explain why we're so adventurous and adaptable as people – and why we've been survivors.

When other New Zealanders witnessed the Pacific migration to Aotearoa in the mid-twentieth century, they were very much inclined to undervalue those migrant families – and underestimate their sacrifices, their courage and their resilience. And, because the newcomers were struggling with English and having to settle for factory and cleaning jobs, they weren't given the respect or admiration they were due. Your parents would've copped those attitudes, wouldn't they? Perhaps your dad especially, with his limited English.

Yeah. But our dad was beautiful with his Samoan oratory and all the stories that he'd recall for us kids. So there was a wisdom and a knowledge he carried that my mum didn't. Or she kind of knew but she couldn't be bothered with it. So they carried different knowledge that we could access.

Actually, we were quite thankful, us kids, that Dad couldn't speak English – even after all these years here. We were grateful because it meant that we had to keep our Samoan language. We could easily have lost it like so many families do when they get too used to speaking English. So we were fortunate we had to respond to Dad in Samoan. It meant that we kept our language and we could understand him and his stories – and some of the beautiful proverbs.

I'm not the one in the family, though, who's good at remembering those sayings and things. My eldest sister, Natasha, is the one who's good with the genealogy and oratory. She's amazing. She's got the memory of an elephant. But not only that. She also understands and can explain the context. It's beautiful. I can sit there and listen to her for ages. She reminds me of our dad. Yeah, it gets me all teary. It's a bit like listening to a chief.

Where do you fit in the family?

There are six of us kids – and I'm the fourth. And, you know, I was a real doongy at school. And I still consider myself a doongy. I wasn't very smart at all. I was terrible. I was even called autistic at times, because I couldn't comprehend what they were teaching. And I hated the English language.

So, it was a real struggle for me – and I became more and more depressed and introverted. And it wasn't until I was a filmmaker, and had to write my stories, that I started to appreciate the English language.

When I look back now at why I didn't really gel with English or understand why we were doing maths, I can see that it's because they were too busy telling us where to put the full stops and the commas. They're too busy doing that instead of getting us to talk about the content and our ideas.

You know. Like: 'Do you have a story to tell? Do you have something to say?' Rather than worrying about the frickin' capital letter and the full stop and the comma. I would've embraced the English language and a lot of the learning a whole lot better if people had just gone straight to the point of why we write in the first place.

Fortunately, though, you survived that school experience – and went off to study drama.

Back in the 1980s and '90s, I ended up on an access course doing a drama module. And I met this amazing man who was running this six-month drama module. It was Rangimoana Taylor. An exceptional man with really artistic siblings: Apirana Taylor and Riwia Brown. Writers. Poets. Performers. Directors. Really brilliant.

And I was this little ratbag. Just eighteen years old. But I did this course and absolutely loved it. And for the first time I was learning something. Probably because it was an art form – and a way of expressing yourself.

Then, at the end of the course, Rangimoana tells me something crazy. He says: 'Sima' – he's got this really beautiful, theatrical voice – 'Sima, you should audition for the New Zealand Drama School.'

So I learned two pieces, auditioned, and got in. That's where my career in the arts got started. And I loved it. But I had so many amazing Māori practitioners, Pākehā as well, looking after me along the way. I didn't ask for it. They just did it. There were no Pacific people around then.

So it was Māori and Pākehā taking me under their wing. Like Colin McColl. He's a good friend now. And Merata Mita, who was like an aunty. Don Selwyn. Barry Barclay. They all knew that I was naughty, but they knew I was the only Pacific person out there, so they just took me under their wing. I was very fortunate to hang out with them and learn lots. I had just so much support and aroha. From Rena Owen and Christina Asher and Whetu Fala as well.

It was pretty cool in those days, touring and doing shows. Quite a few Māori plays. Some of them performed on marae. And I was fortunate that they even considered me, because, you know, when you're brown and you're Pacific Island and there's not many of you, or you're the only one, and you're a woman – well, you get a bit worried. You go: 'Who the heck is going to cast me?' And 'Who would even consider a brown person in their play?'

It was quite scary, especially at the end of drama school. There were five of us brownies. There was me, Hori Ahipene, Cliff Curtis, Julie Edwards and Toby Mills. Five of us. Four Māori and one Samoan. So at the end of the year we were like: 'Who is gonna hire us?' Because we were the biggest brown intake that the drama school had ever taken on.

Then before the year was up, before the graduation, you know, Hori Ahipene and Cliff got roles. Then the other three of us got parts and, for two solid years, I was able to do a lot of acting. Basically at Downstage, Circa and Fortune theatre – and then touring marae. Even doing a sex education show for school kids.

So I got to do all sorts of stuff from Shakespeare to Kiwi plays and Māori plays. But, by the end of the two years, I really wanted to tell my own stories. That's when I started looking for a film school overseas. And I was lucky to find a good one in Melbourne, so I just went for it.

It feels that Māori and Pacific people have, for some time now, been becoming more confident about valuing our own stories – and about deciding to tell them in our own way. No more waiting for the Pākehā mainstream to say: 'Hey, that's a neat story.' And that process is accelerating because of all the emerging platforms – digital and so on.

Oh, it's really exciting. It wasn't this easy in the past. Back in the day, film was a niche little group. Very elite, because making films was so expensive. And it was a real struggle to have your stories told, even in your own language. But now our languages are valued out there because the general public are used to subtitled films after decades of watching Italian, French and Asian films.

And it's to do with film festivals. Film festivals have made non-English films accessible and, in a way, helped Kiwis to be more comfortable with New Zealand films in te reo Māori. In the past, it was hard for Māori filmmakers. They had to get the story right, but then there was the whole thing of whether to translate it into English or have it subtitled. It was a struggle just to get their reo up on the screen because people were going: 'Audiences won't watch that.'

It was really off-putting. Thank God, we're a lot more understanding now. Funders, for instance, are more accepting about having our reo on screen. They realise it can sell – and do really well. And people overseas do want to see our stories.

So the attitudes have changed. Mind you, early on, there weren't that many Māori writers in the industry. Back in the day, there just weren't enough. Now, we've got the Māori storytellers with the confidence to get writing. And more Pacific people are wanting to tell their stories too.

Back a while, we didn't have the confidence. It was like: 'Well, no one is going to be interested in our stories.' But then once films like *Once Were Warriors* and *Whale Rider* came out – bang! That was great affirmation for everyone here that people do love our stories. Here and overseas. They want to see our stories. All types of stories.

And, of our Kiwi films, the biggest box office successes have been Māori and Pacific Island. Not just *Once Were Warriors* and *Whale Rider* but Taika's film *Boy*. And then you've got *Sione's Wedding* and *Number Two*. It just needed filmmakers like Lee Tamahori and Taika Waititi to break out and do something different and amazing.

So now we not only have international people wanting to see our films, but our own people here willing to pay at the box office, and see our films again and again.

ANDREW JUDD
AN UPBRINGING TOO WHITE BY FAR

The former New Plymouth mayor Andrew Judd had an upbringing similar to that of many Pākehā. Like his parents, he never had much to do with Māori. But he didn't see that meagre contact and limited education as any barrier to adopting firm ideas about Māori failings. He now sees those years of uninformed prejudice as a serious mistake, and refers to himself as a 'recovering racist'. But that recovery didn't win him widespread Pākehā applause. Instead, his pro-Māori advocacy was such a bruising experience that he decided not to stand for re-election. He talked to Dale in May 2016.

Andrew Judd: I was born in 1965 and I grew up in Masterton in the Wairarapa. I'm one of six children. Second eldest. Five boys, one sister. My mum's from Guernsey in the Channel Islands. She came out here as a sixteen-year-old with her family after the war. The Germans had invaded their little island – and their house was occupied by a German officer.

Her dad, who was a newspaper typesetter, picked up a job in Masterton for the *Wairarapa Times-Age*. And it was in Masterton that Mum – Jennifer – met my dad, Peter, who was a young, sprightly chap at the local church, St Matthew's. They were both into scouting – cub leaders and then Scout leaders. I whakapapa back to Kent on my dad's side. He ran the YMCA and a menswear shop for many years. But he died when I was a teenager. Mum's still alive. She lives in Masterton.

As kids, we went to Lansdowne Primary School, Hiona Intermediate and then Makoura College.

Dale Husband: *Did you have much contact with Māori in those early days? Classmates? Or teammates when it came to sport?*

There were certainly some Māori children in my class. But no, I never really engaged or connected with Māori. I knew there was a marae at high school, but I never went to it. I'd quickly walk past if I saw anything going on there. I'd look the other way. Never had a need. Not even when I was into Scouts. And I didn't play rugby as a young child – although I did later on. So, no. I had no real contact.

I think that a significant part of the reason for the distance between our peoples is that we didn't interact much as kids. But now, when you look back

*at those years, do you recall any incidents that help
explain your discomfort with Māori – and your
distance?*

There's a couple of things that come to mind.
Once we were driving past some state houses. And
I remember saying to my parents: 'Look, they've
got sheets for curtains.' And they said: 'Don't stare,
Andrew. That's rude. They're Māoris.' I wonder
now what that sort of remark plants in the mind
of a child. I'd bike past other state houses and Mum
would say: 'Make sure your lunch is locked and safe
because it might get stolen.' So, as I'd go past, I'd
speed up. And no lunch was ever stolen. I was never
stopped and harassed in any way, shape or form.

Small examples, but examples of how attitudes
to Māori were planted deep in my psyche. And
there's another shameful example from those
years. Please bear with me. There was a silly
routine as kids when, if you touched somebody that
you thought had maggots, you'd run around and
touch someone else and say: 'I'm fans.' Meaning,
I'm free of the maggots. Then they'd have to touch
someone else to get rid of the maggots. And I
distinctly remember doing that to a little Māori
girl at school. And I think back now: 'How horribly,
horribly cruel. How hard that must have been for
that little girl.'

Yet we thought that game was fun. I reflect on
those times now and I can see that's definitely

where it all started. And, from that point on, it gets reinforced by never having to engage – and never having to see the consequence of those actions. Never knowing how that would have affected her in her life. Never knowing what that behaviour said about me as a kid. Hearing: 'Don't stare. They're Māoris.' Feeling the need to speed up past the state houses. Avoiding the marae. In fact, I couldn't even look at a marae – or the carvings, or the flag – without a sense of fear and anger.

Anger! Why did I get angry about that? What's wrong with me? But, of course, as I now say: 'Well, actually, you're racist.'

It's unusual to hear someone describe themselves that way, because most people are in a state of denial about that. But perhaps we should cut some slack here for you and your folks because, if you haven't met Māori families, if you haven't spent time with Māori people, you'll have a nervousness about that whole scene. There was your mum coming out from England as a sixteen-year-old. She probably never met many Māori. She probably never had any Māori mates. So, that nervousness about an entire people is understandable. We might assume that, growing up in New Zealand, you'll meet Māori everywhere. But there's a lot of Pākehā who never have that contact.

That's right. And Mum and I have talked about this recently. She's one of my biggest supporters. We were a churchgoing family. My dad was a lay

76

minister and my mum sang in the choir. And we just didn't see our attitudes as racism. And she's acknowledged that she just didn't have any Māori friends as a migrant from the UK. And then she went straight into her husband's world.

Okay. So, you're a young fulla. Off to high school. And then off into the wider world.

Well, I didn't feel challenged by school, so I left as a fifteen-year-old and went and worked in a factory, as a cloth-cutter, in Greytown. That was the period when my dad passed away. And, in trying to come to terms with that, I wound up in a flat in Hamilton and working as a cloth-cutter in another factory. Next stop was Huntly where I met and then married Trudi.

Gee, you've gone from one predominantly Pākehā society in the Wairarapa to a very, very Māori scene in Huntly. How did you find life there?

There were two sides to Huntly. You were either an east-sider or you were a west-sider from across the river. But there was a strong connection when it came to sport – and that's when I started having some contact with Māori because I played rugby and cricket in Huntly. But even then, although you'd have a laugh with other players, I never had Māori friends or walked on to a marae. So nothing had changed with me. I still wouldn't look at a marae. I wanted to get past as soon as I could. I'd drive through Ngāruawāhia and just keep driving.

It's bizarre, if you think about it, that I never felt any need to connect. Yeah. Go figure.

Your wife, though, being a Huntly girl, probably had a more thorough Māori 'apprenticeship' than you got in Masterton.

I give a lot of credit to her. All of her schooling was in Huntly, so she had a completely different perspective and world experience than I had. But, through our young marriage and having children, it wasn't something we talked about. My wife's a nurse so, in the course of her training, she went through some cultural training, which I distinctly remember pooh-poohing. I told her I didn't want to hear any of that stuff – or any te reo – around the home. So, she didn't. Then, just a few years ago, she did some reo training. And, once again, I said: 'I don't want to hear that around the house. Thank you.'

When I think back now, my ignorance and arrogance was just mind-blowing. But that's how it was. That's how I was. But she supported me the whole way. She never judged me for having that attitude. And she hasn't judged me now that I've come to realise my ignorance.

Kia ora, Andrew. This is kōrero that I don't hear very much even though I interview many, many people. But let's hear now how you and Trudi moved on and made your home in Taranaki.

Well, I'd started work in the home appliance

world and I got the chance to take over an electric store in New Plymouth. And, 21 years ago, that's where we headed. Sold up everything we had in Hamilton where we'd settled down, and moved to Taranaki. After a couple of years, though, it became clear that the store wasn't the goldmine I'd been hoping for.

So I took on a sales job with The Radio Network. Wrote and voiced a few ads, and did a bit of on-air work. And, in the course of that work, I saw a lot more of Taranaki and got a good perspective on Hāwera and Stratford. But still had no interest in anything Māori. Drove past Parihaka umpteen times. It was just a road sign. Went to Waitara. Never went on to a marae. Nothing. That wasn't part of my world.

You must have been conscious, though, of some of the Māori issues around that time. Māori radio. Māori television. Kura kaupapa. Māori Language Week. All of that sort of kaupapa. Were you conscious of what was going on?

Only peripherally. And the only time I would probably engage with a lot of that was to have a go at it. Maybe I'd be watching the news on Waitangi Day and I'd be thinking: 'What now? How much more of this stuff do we have to put up with? When are they going to move on? I'm sick of this. When are they going to get over it?'

My classic line was: 'Who owns land anyway?

If arriving first means that you own the land, then America owns the moon.' That's where my mind went on issues like that.

Pretty soon, though, you were moving into local government. What was the pathway to that line of work?

Through the radio work, I got to know an optometrist who suggested that I should do some training and become a dispensing optician. That required seventh-form level maths and physics – which I'd been well short of when I left school at fifteen with no School Cert passes. I was quite intrigued and I thought I'd give it a go – even though it meant doing night classes for mathematics and physics.

Funny thing in life is, if you focus on something, at times you can surprise yourself. Which I did. I passed with a distinction. I was really proud of that. And I ended up going out on my own and opening my own practice. I employed optometrists and went on to become the president of our association for New Zealand.

And we had a night here in town where there was a top shop award, and our business won top shop for Taranaki. The then mayor came over and encouraged me to stand for the council. He told me I could be the mayor one day. Apparently he'd say that to everybody. I'd never really given that any thought. But, as you can appreciate, it gets to your ego. You think: 'Yeah, I'll give that a crack. I've got a business. I've got the optics thing going on. Life's going good. I'll give it a crack.'

So I did. And I think I was the second highest polling councillor. And that's the way my local government journey started.

When I got on to the council, we had a komiti Māori. I had never attended any komiti Māori hui at all. In fact, I had to ask one of the councillors: 'What's the difference between a hapū and an iwi? What does that mean?' That's how ignorant I'd been. I'm laughing now at my own embarrassment. I didn't know anything. Nothing. It's amazing, eh? To think you can go through all your life in New Zealand, and not know anything. All I knew was a few words like puku and kia ora – and, of course, some racist jokes. So it was hideous. I look back, and it was just hideous.

But things have changed for you, haven't they? How did that come about?

It was a succession of little things that began when I was elected as the mayor. I'd been in the job for only a month or two when there was a protest out at Waitara about the perpetual leases on Pekapeka block land. So, out I went and heard the complaints from some residents who were concerned that the iwi were getting back the land and were 'going to kick us off'. And there was all that sort of fearful talking.

And I'm driving back to the office, getting into my groove: Enough. Sick of that stuff. I'm the mayor. I'm in a position where I can change that. Enough of this handout. Let's find a way to help those lease holders. This is scary for them, those poor people! Having to go through all of this. Not knowing who the new landlord would be! Oh, no.

Back at the office, the staff gave me the settlement documentation that was going through with the Crown at the time. I opened it up and turned to where Te Āti Awa were talking about the history of the Pekapeka block. *And I got captured by the history*. And before I knew it, a couple of hours had gone past. And I thought: 'I didn't know any of that. Gosh. That's amazing. Why didn't I know that?'

So it sort of chips away at you, these things. You wonder why you didn't know. Then you find reasons to justify why you didn't. You think about how you were raised. So you tell yourself that it's not your fault. That you don't need to feel bad about not knowing. And anyway, you're not Māori.

So there were lots of little steps. And another one was when I was putting together the council committees – and there was the question of Māori representation. We'd always had a komiti Māori. Then the iwi liaison officer told me that the kaumātua would like to meet the new mayor, that's me, at Tui Ora.

And, gosh, I'm thinking: 'What do I need to do?' And they said: 'Nothing. We'll be there to support you.' So I go along to introduce myself. I'm at the door and my heart is pounding out of my chest. Because I look in the room and they're all Māori. Then I thought, so what? Why would that be an issue? Anyway. Stiff upper lip. Be strong. You're the mayor. And I went through and hongi'd right round the room. Sat down and it's all in te reo. I'm thinking: 'What do I say if I have to speak? What do I say? Kia ora? I don't know.'

But what was actually unfolding was a welcome. They were welcoming me. 'We're honoured,' they said, 'to meet you. We are here to work with you and help you where we can. Please stay with us for food and fellowship.'

That was pretty cool. And, when I spoke, I said I'm putting together a komiti Māori. I've come to say hello, and thank you for your warm welcome. In the cup of tea period, some of the kaumātua and leaders said to me: 'Look, with all due respect, we understand komiti Māori but, actually, we don't want it because we're moving from grievance to participation mode. It's just compliance, really. We feel it's not real. It has the same status as your youth committee. Things aren't written. So, with all due respect – obviously you can put it together and you'll find some people that will be on it – but, no thanks.'

You know, that night, sitting back, reflecting on the day, I thought: 'Gosh, they were lovely.' Why was I thinking: 'I'm the only Pākehā in a Māori room?' Why was that even a thought for me? Other than it was fact. But why would I even think that?

In the lead-up to the election, I'd campaigned on doing the right thing. My slogan was: *Let's bring honesty back to local politics*. The message behind that was around finances actually. But, I thought: No. I want to do the right thing on Māori representation. So, a few days later, with some of our in-house people, I met with some of those leaders. I said I didn't want to put a committee together that's not wanted. And I asked them what would work.

Well, their preference was for a Māori ward. But they acknowledged that I'd get a lot of stick if that's what we proposed, so they didn't push for that. They suggested having Māori voting rights on the sub-committees. I would have final sign-off as the mayor, but for them, it would be a step closer to the conversation and decision-making.

But the councillors wouldn't wear that. They said you can't give unelected people a vote. They said that's not democracy. And I heard in their tone, and saw in their eyes, myself. That was the early stages of recognition for me.

So it wasn't on. I thought: What do I do now? Can't have komiti Māori. I can't get representation on standing committees, even though parts of the country have that. What was next? Well, if one option was for a Māori ward, then we'd have elected councillors. Which is what they wanted. So I tried that – and somehow it got passed.

Shortly after, I went overseas, in my capacity as a dispensing optician, for an international optics conference. On the final night, we were asked to come dressed in our national costume – and to do a skit from our country. We were sat next to the Australian table. We were teasing them. Asking what they were going to do. 'Waltzing Matilda'? They said: 'Yeah, well, you're lucky. You've got Māori culture.'

We were all middle-aged, pale, frail cats. And we all got up to do the haka. None of us actually knew how to do it. We just got up and fumbled our way through it. Laugh. Laugh. Chuckle. Chuckle. And teased the Aussies because they just sang 'Waltzing Matilda'.

Flying home I had all that time to think. Okay, Andrew. What is your culture as a Pākehā New Zealander? Because you're not English and you're not Māori. And yet you thought you were justified in grabbing something from Māori culture as yours. Giving it no respect. Not knowing what it meant. Not knowing how to do it. What does that say about you, Andrew Judd?

So that was another step in the journey of

discovering who I thought I was when I was a part of that performance. Then, of course came the journey of the Māori ward. And the pushback. The pushback had me fighting, in a way, against myself. Because everything that was being fired at me was what I used to say. And think. And do.

And it was coming from people I've known for many, many years. People I care about. They were saying what I'd been saying. But I'd been racist. Because the more I was engaging with Māori, the more love I was getting from them. Love.

This, of course, was during the settlement process. I was there at the tail end of that, observing how the Crown was operating with Te Āti Awa. And, of course, I was doing more research and reading. And I became especially interested in Parihaka. So I read Dick Scott's book *Ask That Mountain*. And I was moved to tears.

Why don't we talk about our history? This is bizarre! No wonder I've been like I was. Parihaka has been an inconvenient truth. Not only do we not talk about what was done, but how it was done. Yet we stand on a world stage like we're the be-all and end-all of race relations. No, we're not. We're no different.

So I learn about Parihaka. Then I watch the process with the Crown. Watching how they were just bullies really. And then the settlement process. The signing. The love and inclusion I was receiving from iwi. I was starting to learn correct pronunciation of te reo. I had a lovely lady on staff who said: 'You don't have to, I'm just offering it as a starting point. But, if you want, I can help you with your reo pronunciation.' She just wanted me to stop with the standard Pākehā mispronunciation of Taranaki and Waitara. And I thought: 'Yep. Absolutely.' Because what was unfolding in me was enlightenment.

There are many things that bring us together in New Zealand. And this rich kōrero of yours, Andrew, is part of that. So I thank you for it. But I realise that your principled stand has come at a personal cost to you. I'm disappointed you're not standing again but I can understand that.

What I've found wasn't what I was looking for in my journey as a mayor. But for me, I'm blessed beyond belief. I've found a richness of understanding that I could never have hoped for. I'm not a victim. I've been blessed.

For me, ignorance is one thing. But to realise it and then look past it would be indefensible. So I'm addressing Pākehā. I'm reflecting on what I've been through. And I'm saying: 'We've got it wrong. We're a major part of the problem. We've never acknowledged it because we don't talk about our past. But we need to talk about it in order to understand.'

Taking the land was bad enough. But taking

away somebody's ability to identify with who they are is just plain wrong. We have to change. And it's an attitude change.

If you can identify with what I'm saying, then come with me. And let's see if together we can change this.

NADINE MILLAR
ENDING THE SHAME OF NOT SPEAKING THE REO

Nadine Millar (Ngāti Hine, Ngāpuhi) has a back-ground in journalism and television research, and more recently education, as a policy analyst. When she wrote this, in September 2015, she was learning te reo at Te Wānanga Takiura in Auckland.

A while ago, my husband suggested I learn Māori. We were discussing potential ways I could boost my employment opportunities after four years at home raising the kids. 'How about a total immersion course?' he said. 'You could fast track it and be fluent in a year.'

Naturally, I bit his head off. Only someone who didn't fully appreciate the scale of such an undertaking, the sheer difficulty of learning Māori, would suggest I could become fluent in a year. It wasn't like going to the shops and picking up a loaf of bread. I'd studied Māori at school, done three university courses, been to marae immersion weekends – the works. It wasn't a lack of will holding me back.

'So what *is* the problem, then?' He can be annoyingly persistent, sometimes.

How could I make him understand that my barriers weren't practical, but emotional? A lifetime of feeling like I didn't belong anywhere. Shame was a vine, wrapping itself around my ankles and yanking me off my feet whenever I tried to walk in te ao Māori.

'I'll never be able to speak Māori,' I assured my husband. 'Never!'

But a seed had been planted. I tried not to water it, but it grew anyway. For once, my thoughts about what it means to 'be Māori' embodied visions of the future instead of echoes from the past. I dared to dream about where the language could take me from here. I thought of all the ways te reo Māori complemented my previous study and work experience. I remembered all those work situations where my lack of Māori had held me back. Experiences overseas where people had looked to me for guidance as the only Māori in the room.

And I thought of our children – how they'd learned Samoan when we lived in the Pacific, embraced Arabic while living in the Middle East, yet seemed to look at our own language and culture as something foreign to them.

Suddenly, all my reasons for not learning Māori seemed, well, immature. Blaming an absent parent for my lack of connection to our ancestral lands back home. Equating everything Māori with my own personal sense of loss and dislocation. These were just excuses. It was time to get real.

So, a few months after my husband first suggested I do a total immersion te reo Māori course, I repackaged the idea as my own and presented it to him.

Naturally, he thought it was brilliant.

Ten months down the track, my year of total immersion is winding up. As I look back, I realise I was right and I was wrong. I was right to think of te reo Māori as a key to unlocking an uncertain future, but I was wrong to think that I could move forward without first going back.

In fact, going back was part of the curriculum. Our first assignment was 'Who am I?' and the second was 'Where am I from?' The former involved an emotional journey and the latter a literal one – four hours up north, to Wai-o-mio, the place of the winding waters.

It was a long way to go. Inconvenient, too. The kids fought. It rained. I complained that it wasn't fair to require someone like me, by which I meant 'urban Māori', to embark on a quest to find out the answers to questions that had so far stumped Google. Questions like: 'Where does the name of your wharenui come from?' and 'What is the significance of a whakataukī from your iwi in relation to your marae?'

In the past, assignments for Māori classes had been ticked off with a quick phone call the night before the due date: 'Nan! Quick, what's the name of our mountain?' 'Nan, what's the name of our tupuna?'

But Nan isn't here any more. Her little flat in town long vacated; the homestead, such that it is, occupied by someone I don't know. Anyway, I know what she would have said, because she said the same thing every time I called with these sorts of questions.

'Girl, you just gotta come here and see for yourself. That way you won't forget.'

So, finally, I did. And as I stood on the bank of the river, watching the Taumārere snake a slow, lazy path in front of me, I heard Nan's voice from somewhere on the wind: *Ko Taumārere te awa*. Not a bunch of foreign words any more, but a place where the bend in the river meets the fork in the road.

That pilgrimage back home was a critical turning point in my reo journey. It's the point at which I humbled myself to a process I didn't fully understand. It's not that I was so arrogant that

I thought this thing would be easy. It's that I was so arrogant that I didn't think it would be this hard.

It started right back on day one, when we each had to get up and introduce ourselves to the rest of the class. In a state of panic, I ran through a range of possible ninety-second speeches. I could try a witty approach but worried it might make me sound up myself. I could take a sincere tone, but the last thing I wanted was to come across overly emotional and end up crying.

But, of course, that's exactly what I did. More of a howl, actually.

If there's a comfort zone, studying Māori placed me right outside it. Along with regular public speaking, formally and informally, I have even, God forbid, had to sing. Not just sing, but *compose and sing* my own waiata.

Then there's kapa haka, my enthusiasm for which does not match my ability or sense of timing.

There's also a deep spirituality imbued in everything we do, which my logical side does not always want to engage with, yet without which everything is rendered completely hollow. Karakia, mihi, tauparapara, karanga, waiata, whakataukī. Even, it turns out, tangi. Every emotion has its place in the order of things.

So, that comfort zone? Tikanga Māori placed me right inside it, too. It is the very cornerstone of the language itself. In fact, the greatest gift this year has been the opportunity to put tikanga Māori at the centre of everything I do. To experience a Māori worldview as natural and ordinary, while viewing tikanga Pākehā as something which differs from the norm.

After a week on noho marae I went to my kids' school assembly and felt like I'd just landed on another planet. Where was the greeting to God, to the whare above us, Papatūānuku beneath us, to our ancestors gone to the stars? Who was this person speaking? What was their whakapapa? Were we related or not? Where were the karakia and waiata like bookends, letting us know when one process had ended and another begun?

The whole thing seemed odd to me. When the principal finished addressing the students, I had to resist the urge to break out into a waiata tautoko. It would have been awful, but at least it would have been correct.

I'm six weeks out from graduation, and the only thing I know with certainty is that I still have a long, long way to go. But at least now I know it's possible. I *can* speak Māori. I've found a positive narrative for my Māori identity to replace the one that, until now, had always convinced me that I'd never be good enough. The barriers have gone. I feel like I am right where I belong.

Last week, my niece sent me a text message:

'Quick, Aunty Nadine, I've got to say my pepeha at school tomorrow. What's our river?'

I texted her straight back and told her.

'But you have to come and see it for yourself,' I said. 'That way you won't forget.'

LAURA TOAILOA
JUST BECAUSE SEX IS TABOO, DOESN'T MEAN WE'RE NOT DOING IT

Laura Toailoa was born in Samoa, grew up in Manurewa, and is now living in Wellington. She is 22, and will graduate with a BA with honours in English Literature in May 2017. This piece was published in December 2016.

A few weeks ago, a dead infant was found in a Mangere Bridge reserve. The body of the baby boy, a newborn, was wrapped in old clothes. In the police photos of the clothing, there is a detail of depressing irony: a singlet that bears the words 'SAMOAN CULTURE, OUR PRIDE AND JOY', the brightly coloured print design drowned in dirt and mud.

The image looks like a commentary piece in an art gallery rather than something in the news. But it is. It happened. This is real.

We can't begin a discussion about this single event without considering the wider picture of our attitudes as Pasifika – about sex, pregnancy, abortion, rape and other important and big and scary topics.

For many of us, sex is a sticky topic to unravel and explore. As well as the cultural and religious taboos, our acute awareness of interpersonal space, the vā, makes approaching this topic complicated.

I've seen Pasifika groups and forums try to create spaces and opportunities for open-minded discussions around sex. I even attempted it myself.

As part of my university's Pasifika Students' Council, a friend and I organised an event called *Let's Talk*, to address issues of sex and sexuality for Pasifika.

One of these issues is the reality that, although we may not talk about it, we're still having sex. So how do we ensure we're as informed and as safe as possible?

We made the bold choice to not split the boys and girls into separate rooms. One reason was that we wanted each side to see where the other was coming from. But another reason was that we didn't want those who couldn't comfortably fit into strictly 'male' or 'female' categories to feel excluded from the discussion. We knew that past events *did* split into two, but we bit the bullet and decided not to.

This backfired. A lot of the guys felt uncomfortable and left half way through.

Our theory, which sounded so good in our planning, didn't account for the very real and deep-rooted discomfort and disrespect that comes from approaching these kinds of discussions in this way.

My friend and I had to acknowledge that many Pasifika, even the young and open-minded ones at university, won't be receptive to messages conveyed in styles that go against what they've been brought up to value.

So we failed at finding a more culturally appropriate way to open the discussion. We came in with our enthusiasm, experiences and education, but totally missed the mark about what our peers wanted or needed. We did what we complain Pālagi educators, academics and professional experts do all the time. Assume what they think is best for us and then deliver it without any consultation about what people actually want and need.

But we have to keep trying. We must do better. Urgently.

We need to start talking about short- and long-term contraceptives, abortion, orgasms, masturbation (which girls do, too!), sexual abuse – and what we mean by sexual consent when holding hands and kissing is already incriminating and taboo.

But teasing out our attitudes about these topics is difficult, especially when we've grown up being told to stop asking questions and being kaukalaikiki (cheeky) or fiapoko (smart-mouth know-it-all).

None of this is stopping young people from having sex. Our ignorance isn't bliss any more. It's dangerous. People will only reach out for help if they feel that they'll be supported rather than judged.

I remember once watching *Dirty Dancing* with my mother. I might have been in high school. We talked and laughed throughout the movie, mocking random details. But then came that one heated scene with Baby and Johnny, when she tells him her name is Frances, and he replies: 'Frances. That's a real grown-up name.' And then they do the thing-that-shall-not-be-named.

I swear it felt like eternity sitting next to my mother, frozen in place, not wanting to say anything or even *breathe* too loudly. She knows I know what's happening. I know she knows I know. And yet I sit there and try to contort my face in a way that looks like I've never seen or heard of sex in my whole life.

It's hilarious and ridiculous in retrospect, but I've seen similar stories that my Pasifika friends post on Facebook, about how they, too, feign this ignorance to our parents. Because we've grown up being told not to talk about it, think about it, and especially take part in it.

It makes for funny memes, but this culture of fake ignorance is harming our young people in very unfunny ways. The fact that this is a taboo topic doesn't mean we're *not* having sex. It just means that we hide it, lie about it and aren't properly informed about how to do it safely – physically and emotionally.

When you've been told your whole childhood and adolescence that sex is dirty, it's hard to know how to step into adulthood, and begin to unpick our attitudes and perceptions about sex and everything that three-letter word encompasses.

Some Pasifika youth are surprised at how open I am about my personal sexual experiences and about what I think about female masturbation, and what I've learned after sleeping with people I've loved, and with people whose names and faces I can't recall for the life of me.

I don't mean to be radical about my opinions simply to shock and show how modern and progressive I am. I bare my experiences and opinions because of the relief I've seen in people's eyes, that they're not alone in thinking things they thought were so evil and dirty and thus could never bring themselves to talk about.

I love the feeling of showing someone a health service they didn't know they could access for free, and confidentially. I do it for the handful of those who feel they can't talk about these things with anyone in their family, any of their friends – and who feel too shy to talk to a medical professional.

People, young people especially, often don't get the help they need for fear of being judged or ostracised by the people closest to them. Sometimes people need counselling. Sometimes it's long-term contraception. And sometimes they need to discuss an unexpected pregnancy.

But unless someone has made them feel safe, they won't voice it when they most desperately need to.

My dad once told me that, whatever our family goes through, we'll find a way to make it through. Although we've never had an explicit 'sex talk', that was a small opening to let me know that when push comes to shove, he'll be there for me. More of us need this reassurance.

Although we can only speculate about the circumstances that led to the body of a baby boy being abandoned in Māngere, I can't help but see this tragedy as a symptom (and certainly not the first) of a massive cultural and social problem.

We don't know who disposed of the baby. We don't know if it was lovingly wrapped with tears streaming, or quickly done with a beating heart, afraid to be caught. We don't know if this was done through coercion, or in secrecy. As easy as it feels sometimes, we must resist the urge to jump to conclusions and blame the mother of this baby.

We can see this story as someone else's tragedy. A problem for her family to sort out – the police, the government, the health professionals. Or, as Pasifika, we can accept that she is a part of us. She is our daughter, our sister, our aunty.

And if we want to help her and others like her, we need to find ways to start talking.

VICTOR RODGER
A VOYAGE ROUND MY FATHER

Victor Rodger is an award-winning playwright. He was born in Christchurch and raised by his Pālagi mother and Kiwi-Scottish grandparents. His first play, Sons, *was based on his absent Samoan father. This piece was published in November 2015.*

My father died last week. I was at Carl's Jr. on Queen Street when I got the news. Lady Gaga's ass was hanging out of the sunroof of an SUV in a video on a giant TV screen. Halloween revellers laughed and lurched outside.

I wept over an unopened mushroom burger.

At a small, impromptu service two days later, I was struck by the realisation that none of my friends ever met my father. Yet all of them knew he was a significant figure in my life.

I painted a brief picture of him during the

service, even though my actual knowledge of the facts of his life was scant. He was known most commonly as Tafa, the shortened version of his matai title, Tafa Toa Leulua'i Ali'i. To me he was known as Nick, the shortened version of his name Nikolao. He was from the village of Iva, on Savai'i, Samoa, but raised in Lefaga on Upolu before he moved to Christchurch in the '60s.

By the time I was born, my father and mother were no longer together and he was in another relationship. We never lived together. Ours was not an especially close relationship. But he always made a point of coming to see me every time I stayed with my younger half-brother in Brisbane, where he moved from Christchurch in the '90s.

Since our last meeting in 2012, my father was diagnosed with an aggressive form of Alzheimer's. The occasional photo on Facebook showed a man who was slowly disappearing, a shadow of the robust man I pictured in my mind.

In the end he succumbed, quickly, to pneumonia in both lungs.

If you add up the minutes, the hours, my father and I spent together, I'm not sure that we spent more than a week together. But despite – and more so *because* of – his absence, my father cast an enormous shadow over my life, as inescapable as it was undeniable.

Those who know my work as a writer will know

that the illegitimate-son-absent-father theme is something I have picked over in my work (*Sons*) and returned to again (*My Name is Gary Cooper*) and again (*At The Wake*). A veritable stock-in-trade.

Sons, the play that launched my career as a playwright, was my own version of John Mortimer's *Voyage Round My Father*. It was based on the difficult time I had when, as a nineteen-year-old, I tried to initiate a relationship with my father. I'd heard he was dying and went to see him. I had hated him when I was growing up – but I was taken aback by his charisma and sense of humour.

Having been raised as a virtual Pālagi by my Pālagi mother and grandparents, I found myself trying to negotiate both him and, by extension, the Samoan culture, since both were completely foreign to me. Not only that, but they were minefields, and I stepped on a mine more than once due to a messy combination of teenage self-absorption, cultural ignorance and impatience.

When my father didn't officially and immediately welcome me into his family, I took matters into my own hands. I got to know my half-brothers without revealing my true identity, setting off shockwaves within both our families. It's a decision that I regret to this day.

The first draft of *Sons* was very much a black and white story about goodies and baddies. The villain of the piece was clearly my father.

Life, of course, isn't nearly so neat. Writing *Sons* helped me see my father in a different, less judgemental light. I realised my father was only human. That we all make choices. That those choices have consequences.

Do I hate some of the choices my father made? Absolutely. But do I hate the man himself? Absolutely not. Because, aside from a rare blood-clotting disorder called Antithrombin III deficiency, and an ability to write father–son conflict blindfolded, my father gave me something profound, something that I keep circling back to in these days after his death. My father gave me peace.

Here's the thing. If you grow up with an absent parent, most likely you will occasionally have fantasy conversations in your head. Sometimes those conversations will be accusatory. Sometimes they will be placatory.

But six years ago, my father gave me the fantasy conversation where he said everything I could have ever wanted him to say to me. He acknowledged how my life must have been without him. He apologised.

That conversation was a gift. Because everything I felt, all the anger and hurt and resentment, left me.

For that, I will always be grateful. And for me, that will be his legacy and my testimony.

After my father died, I reached out to Albert

Wendt for a quote. Albert is my father in the literary sense of the word. He came back with this Samoan classic: *Amuia le masina, e alu ma toe sau.*

Envy the moon: it goes and returns.

Unlike the dead.

If my father could come back one more time like the moon, I would thank him. I never did get the chance to in life.

Ia manuia lau malaga, Dad.

KINGI TAURUA
GO AND FIND A PĀKEHĀ NAME

Kingi Taurua has a voice and a face that many New Zealanders, especially those in the north, know well. Much of that familiarity comes from his work as a radio broadcaster and his role as an influential Ngāpuhi leader. But it's also a result of a colourful career: his time as a Northland College flanker in the days when they were holding the Moascar Cup (the high school equivalent of the Ranfurly Shield), and his army days, which had him in action not only in Vietnam but also on duty in the UK, guarding the inmates of Buckingham Palace. There was more duty later, as a prison guard at Paremoremo – and then as a political adviser at the Beehive in Wellington. He talked to Dale Husband in August 2015.

Dale Husband: *Those of us in broadcasting, and many others too, know you as Kingi Taurua. But I understand there are others who know you by another name. How did that come about?*

Kingi Taurua: Well, when I started school at Oromāhoe Native School, the head teacher asked me my name. I told him it was Kingi. He said: 'Now, you go home and you find a Pākehā name – and come back when you find one.'

When I got home, my parents (speaking in Māori, because they didn't speak English) asked me what I was doing home. I told them I needed a Pākehā name. Then a rooster went past – a rooster that one of my brothers had named Albert. So that's what my father named me. And back I went to school the next day and told my teacher my name was Albert. That's what I was called. Named after a damned rooster. So I grew up with that name. In fact, for years and years, I forgot about my real name being Kingi.

When I joined the army, I was selected to go to Salisbury Plains in England for training. I applied for a passport using Albert as my name. Back came Internal Affairs saying there's no one by that name. So I wrote back and said: 'Yes there is. Albert is my name.'

The trouble was that I didn't have a birth certificate, so they asked for my mother and father's name. My father is Te Huhu of Ngāti Whātua and my mother is Arihia, a descendant of Tareha, a chief of Ngāti Rēhia. So the officials checked their records and then said: 'We have a guy here, born on September 3, 1937, and his name is Kingi Taurua. And I went: 'Hey. That's me. That's my real name.' And so I chucked that bloody rooster name right out the window, and I went back to my tūturu name, Kingi.

Okay. But let's go back to the start. Back to 1937. Where did you first see the light of day?

I was born in Oromāhoe, a little village in the Bay of Islands. I caught just the tail end of the Depression. There wasn't much kai at that time, and we were dependent on acres and acres of kūmara, potato, watermelon and corn. And we had coupons for butter, sugar and flour. They were rationed in those days.

My mum would ride into Kerikeri on horseback for those rations each month. That was about a six-hour round trip. Sometimes they wouldn't last until the next lot and we'd be eating rotten corn with our milk – and taking rotten corn for our school lunch. I swore at the time that, when I grew up, I wouldn't ever touch that rotten corn again.

There were ten of us and another ten whāngai stuck in a two-bedroom house. But, although we were short on kai at times, we weren't short on aroha. We had a little farm with five cows. So we milked them, separated the cream and sent it to the factory to generate some income.

We worked hard on the farm, ploughing and

planting. We had bullocks pulling the plough – and later we replaced them with draught horses. There was a very whanaungatanga relationship in the community. My father used to say whanaungatanga meant: 'I am we, not I am I.'

My dad was a veteran of the Māori Pioneers from World War I. But his lungs were gone when he came home, so he spent most of his time in bed. And he died at 52.

Were you one of the rural Māori kids that moved into town?

Yes. I moved down into Auckland, into the city to look for work. Times were tough because there was a lot of unemployment. My first job was on the wharf and we had to start queuing about three o'clock in the morning. There'd be long lines of men hoping to get a job. The boss would walk around and say: 'Yes. We want you ... want you ... want you.' And so on. It was hit or miss. One time, I missed out by one. They just got to me but then didn't need any more workers. So next morning I got there really early to make sure I was in the front of the line.

I used to look forward to the *Tofua* and *Matua* ships coming in from the Pacific islands, because they brought in bananas. When I got on those boats I ate a hell of a lot of bananas.

Next I decided to join the navy but, before I got called up, I saw a sign saying join the army. So I applied there too. And I stuck with the army even though I was also selected by the navy. I was very happy to serve in the armed forces – which I did for about nine years. Most of the boys I served with are dead now. I served in Singapore and Vietnam and other areas I don't want to talk about. I came home as a casualty of the Vietnam War and was discharged in 1967.

And after that? What did you do next?

I became one of the first prison officers at the maximum-security prison, Paremoremo. Mr Buckley was the superintendent at the time. Prisoners were allowed only one book a week. There was no television or radio. Just the bare necessities. Mr Buckley was very supportive of D Block, the maximum-security unit where Ron Jorgensen and John Gillies and all those kind of inmates were held. I worked in that area. And, while I was there, I did the exams in English, psychology, phrenology and public administration – and I became a senior prison officer.

Eventually, I was sent down to Taupō where I was in charge of first offenders at the prison there. After some time in that job, I was shoulder tapped by a guy called John Te Rangihau. He said he'd like me to come to Wellington and help him implement a report called *Puao-te-Ata-tu*, which was aiming to reform the social welfare system. There were a group of us working on that, including Apirana Mahuika.

From there I became an adviser on Māori kaupapa to Helen Clark, Michael Cullen, Annette King and other ministers. Then, when Labour lost the election and Jenny Shipley became the Minister of Social Welfare, I became her adviser for several years. Eventually, she became the prime minister and I left there and came back home.

I'd been phoned by the kaumātua and told to come home. At that time, some of the Ngāpuhi had signed the Sealord deal without the authority of the old people. I was asked to come back and establish the Council of Elders to make sure that the Treaty of Waitangi will never again be torn asunder. So I established Te Taumata Kaumātua, which operated for many years. Most have passed away now. The only guys left are Raumoa Kawiti and me.

One of the many things that make you notable, Kingi, is that you brought the age-old practice of tā moko back to the north. Can you tell us about that journey?

I was working for Ruia Mai in Auckland at that time as a broadcaster when I got a call from Ranga Hohepa, a ninety-year-old lady, saying: 'We need to see you.' I was still the rangatira for the Council of Elders and they wanted me to come to the hui at Kawiti marae. The place was full. I was shocked when the elders said: 'We would like you to take the tā moko.' And I was reluctant to do it because I was a bit whakamā, mainly because I thought people would look at me as part of a gang. So I was very, very reluctant.

Then they had another hui and they brought Eru Morgan and his TV cameras. They were taking pictures of the hui, and so I felt I had to agree. The whole process was filmed. The kaumātua designed the moko, and asked Gordon Hatfield to do it. He and another guy started at five o'clock in the morning and didn't finish until about nine at night. They not only did the moko on my face but also on my backside and legs. That was a long process. They blessed me, and eventually I went home. From then on, I was considered the leader of Ngāpuhi.

It must've been awkward to start. And I imagine you took some time to become comfortable with the moko.

It took quite a while, maybe over a year. Every time I walked past Pākehā people, I looked down towards my feet. I didn't want to see the reaction on their faces. I was whakamā and afraid at the same time of what they might think of me. I had a kōrero with Reverend Māori Marsden about my problem with the moko and he said to me: 'Keep looking up. Don't you look down.' And so I did what he told me – and suddenly my whakamā disappeared and I felt okay.

You've been a very strong advocate for te reo Māori and tikanga Māori, and you've been renowned as a broadcaster for the last twenty or so years. So you must've done some thinking about the role of the reo and the media.

I think a lot of people say that the use of te reo on Māori media is the avenue to identify us as Māori. I recall one time at a hui where a person stood up and spoke in English. And this fulla stood up and said: 'Don't you ever speak English in this marae.'

So I stood up and said: 'Don't YOU blame that person for speaking English. Blame yourself. And me. You and me are to blame because we never, never, never taught them how to speak Māori. It is our fault. I want that person to speak.'

I have aroha for those who can't understand Māori. They are missing out. But you can't wipe their Māoriness away from them. They are Māori. Māori media in both languages is a step forward for those who can't speak Māori.

I wanted Ruia Mai to broadcast in Māori and English and I suggested that. I got told off and I was reminded that it was a Māori radio station and would always only use Māori. When Willie Jackson rang me and said I should come to Waatea, I was so excited I hardly let him finish talking. I came because Waatea was doing both languages.

For me, Māori media doesn't only mean the Māori language. For me, it means speaking in both languages. What excites me is that it is sending out Māori messages in both languages.

SEFITA HAO'ULI
IGNORANCE MAKES YOU EXPLOITABLE

Raised and educated in Tonga and New Zealand, Sefita Hao'uli trained as a journalist in the early 1980s. In those days the media industry was sparsely populated by Pacific Islanders. It still is. But Sefita and other pioneers ushered in an era when New Zealand listeners and viewers became much more familiar with Pacific voices, faces and issues. He talked to Dale Husband in July 2016.

Dale Husband: *Mālō e lelei, Sefita. I understand that you've now spent fifty years in New Zealand. But your origins are strictly Tongan, aren't they? What can you tell us about your early days?*

Sefita Hao'uli: I grew up on the island of Foa, about 100 miles north of Nuku'alofa. My extended family lived in the villages of Lotofoa. For me, as a little boy, those villages were the centre of the universe. Pigs and chickens running wild. Horse riding. And fishing any time you wanted. In many ways, it was quite a rich childhood.

My family had a piece of land where six extended families lived right next to one another. Many villages were made up of twenty or thirty families living close together. Our neighbours were all related, although I didn't realise that at the time.

We lived close to the shore, so the sea was a part of our everyday life. In fact, the sea was our most reliable clock. Often it was our only one, because there weren't many clocks in the villages in those days.

Back in the 1950s, we got some income from copra, as villagers had done for generations throughout the Pacific. It was a sort of cottage industry.

And it meant collecting coconuts, chopping them open and drying their kernels in the sun. If the rain suddenly came, there'd be a panic to get to the shells and turn them upside down so the kernels wouldn't get wet. If they got wet, that would encourage a fungal growth and spoil the quality. So if, say, 400 nuts had been cracked open, waiting to dry, a cloud burst would mean half the village racing out to turn the coconuts over.

And then, when the rain was gone, they'd all race out again to turn the shells over again and expose the kernels to the sun. Then the bags of dried coconut kernel would be sold to traders and shipped off overseas to be made into coconut oil.

Your name, Sefita – where did that come from?

From the Bible. Tonga is a very Christian country and many parents choose their kids' names from the Bible. There's a Sefita somewhere there in the Old Testament. Judges, Chapter 11, as a matter of fact. In English, it's Jephthah. He was a son of Gilead. And, according to the scripture, he was 'a mighty man of valour'. Quite appropriate, don't you think?

The full version of my surname is Hao'uli-ki-namo. But it was too much for the teachers to handle when I came over to New Zealand as a high school student. So it was shortened to Hao'uli.

Hao'uli-ki-namo comes from my father's island, Mo'unga'one, which simply means 'mountain of sand'. A lot of islands are like that. They start out as a reef, then the sand mounts up, creepers begin growing, coconuts floating there from other islands are snared, start growing and, over hundreds of thousands of years, some of these atolls become islands.

Hao'uli-ki-namo means 'to safely surf into harbour'. That was an important skill because our island is surrounded by a reef, so it was a treacherous job making it into the harbour in your fishing boat. You had to wait for the right wave and position the boat outside the break in the reef to take advantage of a big enough wave to sweep you into the shore. That was every seventh wave. Even these days, with outboard motors, it's a tricky and dangerous operation.

You've mentioned high school in New Zealand. I imagine it would've been a huge and probably distressing decision for your parents to send you all this way.

I think they were distressed, but they may have been overjoyed, too. Tongan parents, like parents everywhere, want the best for their children. And in Tonga, that meant striving to get their kids to the 'best' schools. That's quite challenging when you live on a small island, miles from anywhere.

My mum and dad had high hopes for me, so when I was five they sent me to live with my aunt on the island next to ours, because it had a much better primary school. Then, when I was ten, I was sent off to Tonga High School in Nuku'alofa, which was 100 miles south of our island.

Our teachers were mostly New Zealanders or Aussies, and a few Americans. We were encouraged to speak English right from day one. In fact, all our subjects were taught in English. The school was fashioned after King's College here in Ōtāhuhu. So we wore a grey uniform, caps and sandals and, some days, a maroon tie. The girls would wear maroon gym frocks, a panama hat, and sandals as well. The whole concept was of a private school transported across to Tonga.

In 1965, I sat the New Zealand School Certificate exams – and then some of us were sent over here to Auckland Grammar and others went to apprenticeships, such as at the naval base in Devonport. Or to the railway workshops.

I did two years at Grammar and then went on to Auckland University on a scholarship, with the idea that I'd major in geography and then go back and teach at Tonga High School. But they were pretty lax about supervising those of us on scholarships, so I elected to do political science and psychology. And I dabbled in philosophy and education as well, out of general interest.

So you arrived in Auckland in 1966. Was it hard making that adjustment, from Tonga to Auckland?

For us scholarship students, the adjustment was probably easier than for other Tongans. We'd been taught in English by Kiwi teachers so, when we arrived in Auckland, we already knew a lot about New Zealand history and geography.

Every year a group of us would come, and we'd be housed at the hostel at the Tongan royal family's residence in St Andrews Road in Epsom. Our neighbours were some of Auckland's wealthiest families. Like the Caugheys (of Smith & Caughey's). We used to do gardening for them. Some of the boys went to the local Methodist Church in Pah Road, too.

We didn't realise that we were living in a privileged part of Auckland. It wasn't until we were finally invited to Tongan homes that we saw that they lived in these old, run-down little villas in Grey Lynn and Ponsonby, where the houses were all stuck together. Of course, those inner-city villas are now worth millions, but most Pacific Island families moved out in the '70s.

If we move on to the 1970s, we're into the era of the Dawn Raids. What was your reaction to that period?

When we came, there were very few Tongan families here. Before then, few Tongans had passports. It was regarded as a privilege, not a right.

Actually, Tongans weren't encouraged to emigrate at all during the reign of Queen Salote, who was probably our most renowned and loved monarch. She didn't think Tongans should venture out into the world until they were better prepared and, until she died in 1965, the numbers of Tongans moving to New Zealand remained very low.

But, in the 1970s, there was a scheme bringing workers to Auckland on work visas. For Tonga, that set in motion the largest outflow of our population in history. Tongans turned up here in their hundreds.

And, because the scheme was so poorly designed, few of them went home. That was the beginning of the immigration issues and the overstayer phenomenon. The follow-on from that, of course, was the Dawn Raids. And it became very political because National, knowing that most of the overstayers were likely to vote Labour, didn't want them to stay. Labour, of course, did their best to make sure they stayed.

Soon you had Samoan and Tongan lawyers advocating for those who were picked up. And the way New Zealand handles its migrant communities became big news here, and internationally as well. Lawyers like Clive Edwards and Joe Fuimaono made sure that the raids were in the news – and particularly the stories about dogs being used to chase people in Ellerslie, Ponsonby, Grey Lynn and Papatoetoe, and all over Auckland. That was something we still live with today. It's a permanent stain.

And yet, a few years later, you worked for a National prime minister, Robert Muldoon. How did that come about?

Well, that all happened because I became a journalist in the early '80s. I'd been working for the Consumers' Institute, but I was ready for a change – and the opportunity came up to do the six-month journalism course at what is now AUT. So that's what I did.

Looking back, I realise now that journalism was the logical next step for me. Working on consumer complaints had opened my eyes to how New Zealand commerce operates. Some businesses were ethical but others were bordering on the criminal. And Māori and Pacific Islanders were usually the ones getting the rough end of that. A lot of our folks just didn't know enough to protect themselves from the sharks, so they were the bulk of my work. That taught me that ignorance makes you exploitable.

While I was at Consumers, I'd started doing some work for Radio Pacific. That was through a friend, James Waerea, who was looking after the evening programmes. The programmes were in Māori, Samoan and Tongan – and I did the Tongan.

After the journalism course, I was lucky enough to get a job at *Sunday News* when Judy McGregor was editor. She was probably the best editor in the country. But, even though I was barely a year into the job, she recommended me for a position in the prime minister's media office. I didn't expect to get it. For one thing, the job was open to all journalists from INL, which owned the *Dominion* and the *Evening Post*. And, for another, I'd been arrested during the Springbok tour protests in 1981 (while I was doing the journalism course), and ended up in court being prosecuted and fined. I thought my police record would count me out. But Judy said it wouldn't matter, and it didn't. I got the job.

So that was 1983, the year before the 1984 snap election which saw Muldoon out and the Lange Labour government in. Interesting times. What was it like working for someone as feared and disliked as Muldoon?

The thought of working in the PM's office under Muldoon was both exciting and scary. At the time, a lot of the stories that we ran were anti-Muldoon. Of course, it was a rare opportunity to get an insight into how government works. I thought: Why not? I saw it as an adventure.

The staff in the office appeared to live in fear of him. And he was getting a lot of bad press. But he had close support staff who were very protective of him. There were people in the media who had a very good relationship with the PM. However, there were others who the PM had no time for, such as Richard Long of the *Dominion*.

My relationship with Muldoon was cordial and professional. My job was to be there at 8.30 every morning and talk to him about what was on *Morning Report* and in the newspapers. He might ask us to follow up certain stories. The good thing about him was that, more often than not, he'd draft his own press releases.

Because he was PM, you had to treat him with respect, you had to keep your professional distance. And because there were so many people around him, there was very little room for informality. I got to know him better with the trips overseas when there was a smaller group of people.

In the end, there was a human side to him which

I had never appreciated until I was working with him. What I liked about him was that he worked very hard. Most of the time he was the first there, and often the last to leave.

The other thing that surprised me about Muldoon was his sense of humour. He was very funny. Quick-witted. One time, we were coming back from Gisborne. The driver had forgotten to put the New Zealand flag on the car. We were running late, and Muldoon – who was in the front seat, where he preferred to sit – said: 'Driver, would you mind? We need to break the traffic rules to get us to the meeting.' So we were speeding when the driver realised he hadn't put the flag out. He said: 'Oh, I forgot to put the flag on.' We said nothing. When Muldoon didn't respond, he said: 'Prime Minister, would it be all right if I put the flag on?' Muldoon didn't even look up: 'Not while you're doing 110 miles an hour.'

I didn't see or experience any bullying. But he could make things happen promptly. There was one incident where he wanted to see the Minister of Lands urgently. And he kept coming out of his office and asking: 'Well, where is he?' And finally he was told: 'Sorry, Prime Minister, he's climbing in the Southern Alps.' His response was: 'Don't we have any helicopters?' That was in the morning. By about 2 p.m., the Minister of Lands was sitting in his office, still wearing his climbing gear.

The most personal contact I had with him was during the campaign for the snap election of 1984. The chief press secretary, Lesley Miller, decided she was unavailable to do the campaign with him, and he came into the press office and said: 'Sef, I don't have media staff to do the campaign. Would you be available?'

What concerned me most was that you had a prime minister who, at the eleventh hour, had to come and ask for help. I didn't want to be seen as unwilling to help him, even though he was who he was. He was at the end of his career. And, by that time, I no longer hated him as I had at the beginning because of the Springbok tour and because of the way he was as a politician.

I had some compassion for him. He was almost like a caged animal. He seemed alone. I think his lawyer was his closest confidant – he didn't seem to have close friends. His own ministers feared him. His senior members of parliament were looking to dump him. Everybody in the whole country seemed to be expecting his head to roll at any time.

I could see the human side of a powerful person losing his power. At one point in my life, I had considered politics as something I'd take an interest in, but seeing Muldoon cured me of that. If that was life at the top, I didn't want a bar of it. To see a powerful person such as Muldoon and to see how his political life was coming to an end – it's a miserable life being a prime minister on your way out.

On the night he announced the snap election, everyone could see that he'd had too much to drink. Nobody would take the keys off him. He refused the public service driver, insisted he'd see himself home. And, while he was getting ready to go, one of his private secretaries went out and let down his tyres so he couldn't drive.

I was with him for four weeks on the campaign trail. He was behind in the polls and the National Party was in disarray. You could sense that everywhere we went. But he had no regret because he felt he had no option. He knew before the counting started that the election was gone.

After that, you went back to Sunday News. *But then you moved into broadcasting, I understand. First as a news reporter and researcher at TVNZ. Then you put out a Tongan-language newspaper before eventually running the Pacific Island radio station, 531pi, which I suppose was picking up on the work you'd started doing in your Radio Pacific days. How important was the radio station?*

Very important. I felt that the only way to make sure that Pacific issues were clearly understood or told accurately was for us to have a piece of media that would focus entirely on Pacific Island audiences.

And radio was the ideal medium for us. We had seen the value of radio in the Pacific islands where it had become the most powerful medium. More powerful than print. And it appealed particularly in situations where we had multilingual communities. We could divvy up airtime for different languages – you can't do that in a newspaper and hope to be marketable.

What was also clear was that we needed to own the medium. With Radio 531pi, as it was originally set up, the Pacific Island community owned it. It was ours.

It came about when the Lange Labour government sold off the radio frequencies – some of them for millions of dollars. But they held on to three frequencies: one for Māori, which is now Waatea, one for Access radio, and one for Pacific. They flicked it to the Ministry of Pacific Island Affairs on their way out the door.

So MPIA came and spoke to the community. Said they needed some people to take ownership and see how we could make it into something. None of us had any experience of starting a radio station, but we decided to have a go. We formed a community trust, which I chaired.

As we know from flicking around the dial, there are all sorts of approaches to radio programming. But what was your main aim in planning a PI station?

Our idea was that it would inform our community so that life would be better and easier for them in the long run.

That's the transformational power of media. It's to make sure that people are better informed. When you're better informed, you have power. That's the need we were trying to meet for our community.

I became aware of that when I was doing complaints for Consumers and seeing the sad level of ignorance – how ignorance makes you exploitable. It was clear in my mind what the radio station role should be.

With Radio Pacific, we'd had only a few hours in the evenings and that had to be divvied up among so many communities. And you could see that, in fact, the size of the cake also matters. Now we were going to have 24 hours to ourselves as opposed to four hours a week. Or the five or six minutes Radio New Zealand gave us every day. It was a huge jump.

There have been all sorts of developments in PI broadcasting since the days more than 25 years ago when you and your colleagues were setting things in motion. And there have been any number of issues to deal with – funding, ownership, governance, frequencies, networking and programming. Then there's probably been a conflict between the expectations of the PI community and those of the government. Have any of those elements encouraged a change of direction?

The original vision remains. But one difficulty now is that social media has become more and more influential. And some people have been asking why we need radio when we have social media. That line of thinking is, I believe, misguided. In the end, a better-informed community means your sources have to be reliable and authoritative – and you don't get that from social media.

Of course, there's always the option of taking the easy way out. You can sit back and just put music on and say you've got a radio station. But, if your community doesn't know any more after listening to your programme, what use are you?

JOAN METGE
ON MĀORI AND PĀKEHĀ

The racism in Pukekohe more than seventy years ago made a deep and disturbing impression on Joan Metge. She and her family lived there for three years while her schoolteacher dad was first assistant at Pukekohe Primary during World War II. That experience set her on a path to learn (and then teach) what she could about Māori communities, which were so close and yet so foreign to Pākehā. Her work has helped many New Zealanders become more attuned to, and embrace, the different ways we live our lives. It has led as well to widespread respect and affection for her – and to a range of awards and honours. She talked with Dale in June 2015.

Joan Metge: I have always proudly carried the name of Pākehā because my Māori friends use it to identify those people, mostly of British descent, who have put down their roots in this country.

My parents, often, would use the term 'Home' – and you heard the capital H when they talked of England. I used to challenge them about that. Silently at first and, later, quite openly. To me, this country, Aotearoa New Zealand, is home. I belong here and my identity is a marriage between my Scottish, Irish and English ancestry and my personal friendships with tangata whenua, with Māori. I claim that I belong here as much as they do, even if I can't claim the same length of whakapapa connection.

Dale Husband: *Can you tell us a bit about your parents and their background?*

My father was Cedric Leslie Metge. Centuries ago the Metge name was French. An ancestor fled France at the time of religious persecutions and went to Ireland where there was already a group of Huguenot refugees. And my grandfather came to New Zealand from a town called Navan, northwest of Dublin.

My mother was Alice Mary Rigg. Her mother, Clara Partridge, came from Stroud in Gloucester-shire. Clara's father must have been an upwardly mobile tradesman because he was adamant that none of his womenfolk were going to go out to work. She didn't agree with that. She had a mind of her own. She wanted to be a nurse so, the day she was

21, she left home, went to London, did her nursing training there – and met my grandfather who came from Cumbria, near the Scottish border.

My parents met through teaching. My father was teaching at an Auckland school when my mother, who was several years younger, arrived as a trainee teacher 'on section'.

In those days, you didn't marry promptly. They were engaged for three years and didn't marry until my father was appointed as the headmaster at Tauraroa School just south of Whangarei.

Seeing that both of my parents were teachers, my sister Dorothy and I grew up in a home focused on learning. But higher education was almost an impossible dream in those days. So when I finally got to university, I spent the first week there walking at least a foot off the ground.

Now I look at my grandnieces and nephews who take their right to go to university entirely for granted – and I think: 'You don't know how lucky you are.'

I understand you spent your early years living in Pukekohe.

Actually, I spent my first ten years in Auckland. These were the Depression years, so life was pretty constrained. My father's salary took one cut, if not two, in that time. And, on the horizon, there were war clouds which finally broke just about the time we moved to Pukekohe.

When we finally got a house there, it was outside the town limits. Across the road it was all market gardens. And that was my first … well, I won't say 'encounter' with Māori, because it wasn't really an encounter. But I saw those Māori workers in the gardens at a time when there were no trade unions for migrant workers.

They were seen as rather feckless drifters. And there were no bylaws to govern the obligations of owners to provide proper housing and so on.

So I had an early and shocking encounter with the way we can treat our fellow human beings. Most of the workers on the gardens were Māori. And it was sort of received wisdom among the Pākehā that they all came from elsewhere. But, years and years later, I found out that many of them were, in fact, the descendants of the previous owners of that territory.

It was in Pukekohe that I saw a very real social and economic divide between Māori and Pākehā. But, at the same time, I had the opportunity to make personal friendships.

My best friend at school was Eileen Yate who came from the gardens. Her mother was Māori and her father, Willie Yate, was Chinese.

We had a Māori curate at the Anglican Church in Pukekohe and every time I have to define aroha I think of him. Aperahama Kena. He was the most outgoing, generous and loving man.

And we also had occasional visits from Mutu Kapa from Te Aupōuri in the Far North. He was the pastor for the Māori community in Tūākau. Whenever I think of the word mana, I think of him. He had an innate dignity, secure in his own identity. He treated everyone with great courtesy.

I think those Pukekohe years, in all sorts of ways, were crucial because they showed me that there was another world apart from the monocultural Pākehā world in which I'd grown up to that point.

We left Pukekohe and went to Matamata at the beginning of secondary school for me. And that was also very interesting because there were a number of small Māori communities in the surrounding country which, in many ways, were isolated from the rest of the population.

So I didn't really have any Māori friends in Matamata. But it did start me off with an interest in the history of the Waikato, especially the Land Wars and the outstanding leaders like Wiremu Tamihana and Rewi Maniapoto.

Sadly, a lot of Pākehā have grown up in circumstances where they haven't made Māori friends, where they haven't been to their houses, or visited marae. But the contact has become more commonplace, hasn't it? And bicultural relationships may not sit quite so comfortably in many other parts of the world.

We like to boast about having the best race relations in the world. And it's true that we have come a long way in my lifetime. But, during my growing up in Pukekohe, things were very far from perfect.

The middle-class Pākehā living in Pukekohe were good-hearted in many ways, but they were involved with their own lives and with fighting the war. The problem, now as then, is that when we know only one culture and one language we live in that world, like fish live in water, taking it for granted that this is the way that things are, and this is the way things ought to be – and we have a shocking history of imposing that very ethnocentric and, ultimately, very arrogant view on other people.

My life has been a process of finding out to what extent we have done that to Māori. I can remember reading Dick Scott's book *The Parihaka Story* (the first version of *Ask That Mountain*) and I was utterly shocked at what had happened in my own country which I had believed till then had always adhered to the rule of law and to justice.

As I said, we have come an unimaginably long way from where we were when I was young, but it's important that we acknowledge what has happened in the past.

Part of the reward of making Māori friends is finding out there are two sides to our history. There's the bad side but also the good side, the friendships, the partnerships, the long-standing relationships – and, of course, the marriages that have arisen as a consequence.

As you look back now on the life you've led and on the research you've done, how do you feel about having taken the opportunities to see and understand some of the dynamics of a Māori world that few of your contemporaries have shared?

Well, at Pukekohe I had the feeling that there was a whole world, a Māori world, of which I only had glimpses. And not only did I want to know something about that, but I realised that other Pākehā like me needed to know much more, because we were ignorant. That was the motivation that took me to university.

I went there to study anthropology. But, although it was on the books, anthropology wasn't actually being taught. So I ended up doing degrees in geography. I saw that as laying the groundwork for personal encounters which would open up the Māori world, and for finding out what was going on in the present.

At that time there was a lot of talk about Māori urban migration, and almost everybody – Māori elders and politicians anyway – talked about it in negative terms, using words like 'drift' as if the migrants didn't have good reasons for migrating.

There was an awful lot of people making generalisations and I wanted to get to the heart of it.

But nobody was talking to Māori, to the people involved, to those actually moving to the city.

So my first research was done in Auckland, in the central city streets lined with apartment houses and in a rural community up north. And I didn't look beyond that immediate task. I just saw it as something that needed to be done. And I found that it was confronting and difficult, but very rewarding.

I couldn't have managed it without scholarships. Then I went overseas to London and wrote it all up as a PhD thesis, under the eye of Raymond Firth, a New Zealander who had come from a South Auckland farm (called Ōtara), where Ōtara was later established.

I could have stayed in England and been an academic, but I've never seen myself as an academic. I've always seen the pursuit of knowledge as a means to an end. And, when I came back, I was unemployed for several years. I survived with the help of a Carnegie scholarship to do some social science research, and then got a job in Adult Education, a branch of the university concerned with outreach to the general community.

And there I was privileged to work with Matiu Te Hau, Maharaia Winiata and, later on, Koro Dewes.

I was teaching courses on Māori society and culture – not as an expert on those subjects but as a sort of conduit where I could pass on what I'd learned to other Pākehā.

No doubt there was some Māori opposition to the role you were playing?

Yes. There were Māori who felt that Pākehā should keep their noses out of Māori research. But my argument has been that I (and other Pākehā) know what we need to tell other Pākehā because we know what they don't know.

The opposition and challenges I faced from a few Māori were more than outweighed by the cooperation and aroha of the many. The more I have listened and learned, the more I have come to understand the anger and to appreciate the patience and graciousness of the majority.

TERESIA TEAIWA
YOU CAN'T PAINT THE PACIFIC WITH JUST ONE BRUSH STROKE

Teresia Teaiwa is a poet, award-winning teacher and head of Victoria University's Va'aomanū Pasifika (Pacific Studies). In October 2015, she talked to Dale Husband about the complexities of the Pacific – a region with 1,200 indigenous languages and 20,000 islands spread over a third of the earth's surface – and her own complicated cultural heritage as the child of an African American mother and a Banaban and I-Kiribati father whose community was relocated to Fiji because of British phosphate mining.

Dale Husband: *Teresia, a nice place to start, often, is names. So could you tell us about your whānau, your aiga, your mum and dad, and where you were when you grew up?*

Teresia Teaiwa: I was born in Honolulu, Hawai'i, but I was raised in Fiji.

Teaiwa is my grandfather's first name. In Kiribati (pronounced Kiri-bas) it wasn't customary to have last names. That was a colonial introduction. So my father took his father's first name as his last name. My father is John Teaiwa. John wasn't his birth name – that was the name the priest gave to him when he went to school.

Teaiwa is a name from the island of Tabiteuea in Kiribati, which is the largest island in the Gilbert Islands group. Teaiwa is composed of *te* meaning 'the', *ai* meaning 'fire', and *wa* meaning 'canoe'. I like to interpret it as *the fiery canoe*. But when you look for the word *aiwa* in the dictionary, it has a less poetic rendering – agitation is one of the interpretations that comes to mind.

Tell us about your folks. What were they involved in?

My parents were both studying at the University of Hawai'i when they met. My mother, Joan, is African American from Washington DC. She moved to Hawai'i to do her masters in teaching English as a second language. My father went to Hawai'i as a Fiji scholarship student to study agriculture.

Three generations of his family – his grandfather, his parents, him and a couple of his siblings – were relocated to Fiji after World War II with their whole community from the island of Banaba in Kiribati, because the British wanted to continue mining their island for phosphate.

So, that's how we came to be in Fiji, because of the phosphate mining. My dad, from the age of six, grew up in Fiji. I was born in Hawai'i, then we moved back to Fiji in 1969.

My mother was a high school teacher, first, and then lectured at university for a while before working as an editor and course developer for distance learning. My father rose through the ranks of the civil service, eventually retiring at permanent secretary (CEO) level.

Teresia, cross-cultural marriages are not uncommon in New Zealand, but in that Pasifika setting, was it acceptable? Did it at times create some problems?

There were a few problems. In the Pacific Islands there have been cross-cultural relationships ever since contact with Europeans. And, of course, Pacific people have been mixing among themselves for millennia. But I guess what was unusual at that time in the 1960s, early '70s, was that my father married an African American. Didn't marry a Pālagi – didn't marry someone white. And so that was different.

Fiji was a British colony at the time. And unlike other British colonies, Fiji had actually petitioned to be colonised. So there's a very fierce kind of loyalty that indigenous Fijians have toward the British. They very much identify with the British Crown and with English culture.

And one of the things my mum found was that, in the early days, the racism she experienced, as someone of African American descent, was not from white people – there weren't actually that many white people around – but from indigenous Fijians who thought she was inferior because she was descended from people who had been enslaved.

So that was a really difficult dynamic for her. And also ironic, because my mother is a light-skinned African American with blue-grey eyes.

But my mum's lived most of her life in Fiji now, and Fiji's become home. She's really comfortable there now. And she often gets mistaken for being Fijian herself.

I notice you don't use the term 'black' when describing your mum, that you use African American. I just wonder is the term 'black' something you'd rather not use?

No, I'm fine with black. But I'm careful when using it. I don't mind using black for myself because I *am* black. (*She laughs.*) I'm dark. Whereas, if I told people: 'Oh, my mum's black', and then they met her, they'd be like: 'Hey, your mum's not black.' But if I say my mum's African American, then the rainbow of colours is open to us.

The light-skinned people in my mum's family deliberately chose to identify as black, as African American. They never tried to pass as white. When I'm speaking to people who aren't African

American, I use the term African American. But if I was talking with other African Americans, I wouldn't have to use the term.

It bothers me when New Zealanders use the term 'negro' and when Polynesians use the other 'n' word – it drives me wild. I've taught my sons not to use the word. It's an insult to our African American ancestors.

Our thinking about race is very complicated in the Pacific. I've always been fascinated by that historical moment, in the 1970s and a little bit into the 1980s, when Māori were really embracing of the term 'black', especially the Māori feminists who called themselves black feminists. And it's also interesting that it has passed, and, for Māori now, it's like: 'Oh, we're brown.' The colour politics have shifted.

Being born in Hawai'i, did you ever feel that Americanism had suppressed Hawaiianism?

Absolutely. The years I lived there while I was doing my masters were really intense because that was 1989 to 1991. The Hawaiian sovereignty movement was really building momentum, and I had the amazing good fortune to be able to study with Haunani-Kay Trask, who was one of the catalytic figures in the sovereignty movement at the time.

Hawai'i was incorporated into the US as the fiftieth state, when it really should have gone on to the UN decolonisation list. The vote for statehood that took place in the late 1950s never had the option for the people of Hawai'i to become independent.

A lot of people forget that when Pearl Harbor was bombed in 1941, Hawai'i wasn't an American state. It was a colony – a territory. It had been annexed illegally to the United States.

Up until 1893, Hawai'i was a sovereign monarchy. It had embassies all around the world. It had its own currency, it had its own stamps, and was a fully functioning modern state. 'Iolani Palace had electricity before the White House and Buckingham Palace. So Hawai'i was sovereign, it was independent, it was modern. And unfortunately, now, as a result of American colonialism, native Hawaiians have some of the worst health and social indices in the United States.

With your connections to Kiribati, the story of that and the sadness on Tarawa is something I just can't get out of my head. All of those American soldiers who fell, effectively defending the Pacific. I wonder whether you have angst toward the Japanese. I had a high school teacher whose husband couldn't bring himself to buy a Japanese vehicle because of what he'd witnessed in the Pacific during the Second World War.

My background is in history, and one of the things I try to do as a historian, even though it's difficult

– I try to encourage empathy in my students. And what that means is, try to put yourself in someone else's shoes.

So, it's true that during World War II there were great atrocities that the Japanese were responsible for, and certainly on my island of Banaba, when the Japanese landed, they executed a number of our people.

But I also know, as a historian, that where Japan already had some Pacific colonies – what's now the Federated States of Micronesia – and even in their encounters with people in Papua New Guinea and the Solomon Islands, the Japanese made friends.

For me, it's complicated. I want to hold Great Britain to account as much as I want to hold Japan to account for what happened to Kiribati. As someone whose island was mined by the British, almost making the island unliveable, and whose whole community had to be relocated to Fiji, thousands of miles away, I thought when I was growing up that I should hate the British.

And then I had an opportunity to study in England, and when I got there, I realised, well, British society is really complex. There were old white people who were really kind to me. And there were awful young people – skinheads – who were terrifying. And there were so many Indian, Pakistani and African Brits.

And then I realised, wow, you can't just paint one

brush stroke over a nation and say that's who they are. The young skinheads – they didn't mine my island, but the hate and the disregard they showed was similar to that demonstrated by some of the people who mined my island. By the same token, there were good people in England who didn't know what this company, the British Phosphate Commission, was doing.

You've lived in some pretty volatile communities. What was it like growing up in Fiji?

Because of my father's postings through the Ministry of Agriculture, we got to live in different parts of Fiji, from Nausori to Savusavu, Levuka (the old capital) and Lautoka, before we finally settled in Suva.

For me, this meant going to schools in all these places and, as a result, having wonderful friends and very special memories from across the country. We lived in Savusavu from 1973 to 1974 and I didn't go back until 1996, but when I did, people recognised me even though it had been almost twenty years since I had last been there. That's what I love about having grown up in Fiji. Fijians attach tremendous importance to human relationships, and their memories for faces and names are incredible!

That hasn't changed after all the political turmoil that the country has been through with four coups since 1987, but I would say there are more and more people falling through the cracks with increasing urbanisation, growing disparities between the very rich and the very poor, and rising rates of violence.

An unintended outcome of the coup culture and political instabilities is that there is a robust civil society – lots of NGOs, quite politically engaged churches, and growing confidence among young people in terms of political participation and commentary, especially through social media.

If there's one thing that coups have done for people in and from Fiji, it is that they have made the concept of 'democracy' less abstract and distant.

What did you do after university in Hawai'i?

I went on to do my PhD at the University of California, Santa Cruz. I followed another University of Hawai'i graduate, and after me a whole string of other Pacific scholars came along in our wake.

Because our PhD programme specialised in critical theory and cultural studies, a lot of the Pālagi academics who were used to being unchallenged about their expertise on the Pacific often described us dismissively (and erroneously) as 'postmodern'.

But the reality is that a small number of academics at the University of California, Santa Cruz, produced more confident, creative and activist Pacific PhDs in a twenty-year period than any southern hemisphere university had. And some of us came back to the Pacific to kick arse and show our people that we can engage at the highest levels of education and that pursuing intellectual self-determination is not only possible, it's necessary.

You're here in New Zealand now. How did that come about?

I was the first academic hired when Pacific Studies was founded at Victoria University in 2000. This was the first university in the world to establish Pacific Studies as a major in the BA degree.

After an international search, I was appointed the first lecturer, and I started in 2000, teaching all the courses. Three years later, we were granted another full-time lecturer position, and now Pacific Studies has expanded to offering a BA Honours, MA and PhD degree as well. We had our first PhD in Pacific Studies graduate a couple of years ago, and by the end of this year we will have four PhDs graduating, which is pretty remarkable for a programme with a full-time academic staff of 2.5.

I think you'll find in a lot of organisations around New Zealand that Pacific programmes and staff punch above our weight. We have learned to make the most out of the little we are given.

But we can never take for granted that universities will be committed to having us, and supporting us. We have to keep proving that we're relevant – not just locally, but internationally. So, part of my sense of responsibility as an academic is getting my colleagues, and my students, to publish in international venues – to get our kōrero out to global audiences – so that we're protected at home.

But also, we understand that the work we're doing is not just important for our people, but important to other people in other parts of the world. We have something to teach the rest of the world as well.

I'm curious. When you talk about Pacific Studies, do you factor the Māori story into that? Is it all of us in the same waka together?

Pacific Studies was first housed in Te Kawa a Māui, which is the school of Māori Studies. So that's a really important part of our whakapapa at the university.

Even though Māori Studies exists as its own discrete area of study, we can't do Pacific Studies without acknowledging our location, and that our own location in Aotearoa has its own indigenous histories, and that those histories are Pacific.

Māori are integral to our story. If you did Pacific Studies in Hawai'i, California or Fiji – Māori are always considered part of Pacific Studies. But it's only when we're here in Aotearoa, we have to conscientiously think about this relationship between us as *tagata o le moana* (people of the sea) and *tangata whenua* (people of the land).

How well are Pacific students doing at university?

In 2014, our undergraduate students in Pacific

Studies were achieving at rates 10 per cent and even higher above the overall rates for Pasifika students across the university (78 per cent compared to 68). By comparison, the overall rate of achievement for all students at Victoria that year was 88 per cent.

In some of our courses the failure rate for Pacific students can get as high as 25 per cent. That's really alarming when you think about how these students are putting themselves into debt to the tune of around $1,000 per course, and if they fail, they still have that debt even though the course will not count towards their qualifications.

A lot of our Pacific students straight out of high school are not emotionally prepared for the kind of independent learning you need to be hungry for at university. Our young people are used to being disciplined by their parents or high school teachers – most of them have not yet developed internal discipline and motivation for themselves.

Sometimes I think it would be better for some of our students to have a gap year, or take a break from institutionalised learning and get some life or work experience before coming to university. But there is a lot of pressure from parents, extended families and church communities – whose sacrifices for their children can paralyse rather than motivate them. It's tough, and sometimes students crumble under the weight of such expectations.

You've won a number of awards, including the

Ako Aotearoa award for Sustained Excellence in Tertiary Teaching last year. Many of your students have also commented on how inspirational and life changing it's been having you as a lecturer. How does Pacific Studies help Pacific students?

Pacific Studies helps a lot of Pacific students to experience for the first time how academic learning can be dynamically engaged with who they are, where they are from and where they live. Many of my students had not been exposed to the writings of Pacific authors before coming to university, and our introduction to Pacific Studies course helps them trace an intellectual history of the Pacific that many of them did not know was there.

University learning can be alienating, so when students find their feet in a knowledge base that not only stimulates them mentally but touches them spiritually, it gives them the confidence to tackle the knowledge that they will encounter in other disciplines. For me, it's gratifying to see students who excel in our classes go on to excel in other courses. It becomes a virtuous cycle.

How do you think PI communities in New Zealand are faring?

I think PI communities in New Zealand are in an interesting moment. Politically and culturally, there's a strong sense that this country has been good to them, or good for them. As a relatively recent migrant, I can see that.

But it also feels like PI communities are a bit lost at the moment – all the successes and gains that have been made in politics, sports, the arts and entertainment have not eliminated ongoing problems in health, education, employment.

It's not clear who our real friends are any more – which political parties or institutions we can rely on to champion us.

Is there anything you'd like to add, Teresia?

There are so many issues that are pressing, urgent and, actually, that the rest of the world is watching us on. Climate change is one. I have a lot to say about climate change. But there's also a way that I feel that climate change is colonising the Pacific and people's imagination of the Pacific. And, as a Pacific Studies teacher, that's what I resist. I'm constantly resisting other people's attempts to reduce the Pacific to one thing – to one issue. Whether it's climate change or their relaxing holiday in Fiji. I want to disturb all that.

For us, it's never one issue. We live complicated lives. We're constantly having to negotiate different challenges. And that's my job as a Pacific Studies academic. It's to raise those things. It's to remind people of the complexity and not let them try to paint us with a single brush stroke.

JIM BOLGER
MAYBE THE UREWERA
OWNS ITSELF

Jim Bolger was prime minister of New Zealand from 1990 to 1997. In this revealing interview with Wena Harawira, published in May 2016, he talks about Treaty issues and Māori development. Excerpts of the interview were screened by Māori Television's Native Affairs programme in April 2016. Wena (Ngāi Te Rangi, Ngāti Ranginui, Ngāi Tūhoe) caught up with Jim at a meeting of the Crown–Tūhoe board, which now manages Te Urewera. Wena started by asking him what skills he brings to this board.

Jim Bolger: I guess my skills are somewhat obvious in the sense of the senior positions I've held from prime minister down. But what's more important is the attitude I bring to the board because, if we're going to be successful and take through this new concept of the Urewera 'owning' itself and having its own legal personality, it's going to be dependent on the views and values of the board members.

Wena Harawira: *Has Tūhoe contributed to your knowledge of things Māori? Or changed your perceptions of Māori?*

Every time I've engaged with Māori over the years I've gained new insights and new perspectives. Different iwi will have their own perspectives. But I've had the good fortune to grow up in a community where there were a lot of Māori people. I went to school with Māori. In fact, I was taken to school with Māori neighbours because they had a car and we didn't. So I've had that engagement through the whole of my life. Therefore, I'm comfortable with it.

But I realise how little I know about particular aspects of Māori thinking, history, mythology – and what really drives Māori. Things that perhaps we don't see on the surface.

My wife Joan went to school with the children from Parihaka and I went to school in the village next door, Ōpunake. And the sad thing is that, while we knew it was a unique pā and there was some obviously unique history, we weren't taught that at school.

Such a rich vibrant story and yet we were taught about the War of the Roses. We had a very strange perspective as to what was important.

I grew up close to Parihaka and knew about the great chief Te Whiti o Rongomai who said: 'No, we're not going to fight. There's enough land to share. Why fight?' But we didn't listen. We would've been much better people if we had. This was a man who was years ahead of his time. He was ahead of Mahatma Gandhi, the pacifist leader of India's independence. And ahead of Martin Luther King in the United States with his pursuit of civil rights and non-violence.

How has it been working with Tamati Kruger who led the Tūhoe negotiations?

Tamati has a very deep philosophical view of the world. You have 'life force' discussions with Tamati.

This whole idea that the Urewera owns itself is a concept that looked totally radical and off-the-wall. Unlike the Pākehā view that everybody owns something. But we discuss the issue of the land having been there forever. So it owns itself. And our responsibility is a version of kaitiaki.

Clearly, Tūhoe carry that mantle and the board carries that mantle in a slightly different way. How do we, on behalf of all New Zealanders, not only Tūhoe but the wider New Zealand community, carry that mantle of caring for – and being respectful of – the Urewera? In a sense, it's a matter of being humble in the face of its greatness.

These are totally new concepts. In one way, I can see them fitting in quite easily to the whole environmental movement worldwide. It's just that the human population hasn't been respectful enough to the land, the water and the atmosphere. We've always just presumed it was always there, forever, and it was unlimited.

The colonial mindset, when they left Europe and other countries, was that, when they ran into land somewhere and stuck their flag on the shore, they could go forth and exploit. The land was unlimited. Now we all know land is limited and already severely damaged. So we have a responsibility to care for it. We have to manage things differently. We have to change.

Shall we turn now to Treaty settlements? Are you finding that the New Zealand public is becoming more receptive to the settlements?

We still have a selling job to do. I had a difficult selling job when I started what I describe as the modern settlement process. In other words, seriously looking at what we should do to settle the grievances that came out of our colonial past and subsequent to that.

People aren't going to line up in the street and applaud and say: 'What a wonderful idea.' But I have great respect for New Zealanders. They are decent people who'll behave decently if the arguments are put forward in a sensible fashion and the explanations are given.

Just recently, we had this terrible statement from the Secretary for Education that they weren't going to teach the history of the New Zealand

Wars in our school curriculum, because it would somehow upset the scheme of things.

But we absolutely must teach an honest history of the settlement period of New Zealand. That's the only way you can get acceptance of what still has to be done to correct some of those errors of the past. It wasn't this generation that caused them, I know. But it's this generation that has the responsibility and the obligation to resolve them. It can't be handed on to another generation.

How do you feel about the Treaty process today?

I think we're doing some good. I could argue that we could do better or go faster. But, in some respects, speed shouldn't be an issue. That's something I've learned from interacting with Māori – Māori leadership. It's getting it right that's the important issue.

I get frustrated at not getting up to speed quick enough. Then I reflect and say: 'Well, it's been there for more than a hundred years, so what's another year?' It's disappointing that some people are missing out. But you've got to try and get it right.

The progress through the 1990s was very positive. Then there was a bit of a lull. We've had three good Treaty Negotiations ministers – my good friend Doug Graham, Michael Cullen and Chris Finlayson. They all have empathy for the issue.

That work can only be done by people who have an openness of mind and heart, and who can see the issue through the eyes of those who were oppressed – and then ask: 'How can we address that?' We can't go back to what existed before. So we need to look at what is reasonable for this generation to do. Then we should get on with it.

Fair and reasonable compensation has been a contentious issue. Has this caused the government and Māori to look outside the box with the settlements?

Ocean fisheries was the first big settlement I did. I consider that to be successful and innovative. We know now that we have to manage the oceans and sustainable fisheries because most of the world's oceans have been over-fished. And we know now that the vast Pacific Ocean is actually a limited resource. That's tested the durability of that settlement. But it also developed our thinking in a new way.

Tainui demonstrated the importance of two things. As land was taken, land must be returned. The other was more challenging and interesting. As Tainui had been – I use the word – *insulted* by the Crown, the Crown had to apologise. Now that's a challenge, seeing that the Crown's Head of State lives in London.

So what we did there – that's myself, Doug Graham and Foreign Ministry officials – was to reach out to the palace and say: 'We will write a very detailed and substantive apology in the introduction to the Act that settled the Tainui claim, and invite her Majesty to sign that Act into law on her next visit to New Zealand.'

That was a first. That was innovative. And that got past an obvious block because you can't just roll on to the palace and say: 'Sign here, Ma'am.'

I have this wonderful photo of me with my hand out inviting her Majesty to sign there.

Why did you go for a billion-dollar cap to settle all the historical claims?

That was the first challenge when I was prime minister. What was a fair amount? So I set a billion dollars. Some said that's outrageous. That's an extraordinary sum of money. I could not even pretend I had calculated all the potential claims and come to a sum. Nor had my colleague, Doug Graham.

We just agreed that a billion dollars was a large sum of money and we had to have some parameters to encourage the early settlers, Tainui, Ngāi Tahu and so forth, because they had to have some idea of what the Crown's thinking was. It has since gone much higher than that, which was almost inevitable.

There's been a tendency for the public to keep referring to the settlement payments as 'taxpayers' money'. But that's wrong, isn't it?

Yes. But the good news is that, as we've progressed and we've demonstrated the benefits of settling, New Zealanders, I think, have almost universally come on side. Of course, you get some that aren't on side – but that's inevitable.

But there is no drama now when the government announces a settlement of an iwi claim. And that's a wonderful transition for New Zealanders over the last twenty-odd years. They have moved from saying: 'There is no difference between us, and there's nothing to be done' – which was the common view – to saying: 'We seem to be doing it right.'

So people have a better understanding today of the Treaty process?

Our history is the key. You've got to understand history and that's why we've got to change this view about the Land Wars.

Does the Treaty process have a bearing on New Zealand's race relations?

Absolutely. My view is that it has a very positive bearing. Fair-minded people can see that progress has been made. This is not something that's been brushed to one side and ignored. It's now been brought together in a way that's reasonable and fair.

All New Zealand has an interest in this being resolved. We have to deal with some of the errors, mistakes and abuses of the past. And that's what we're doing.

Who were your Māori mentors when you were prime minister?

I spoke with a lot but I think of people like Sir

Graham Latimer from Ngāpuhi, who I knew before I was PM. He was always a wise calm head. Sir Tipene O'Regan was another. I had a lot to do with him in my time in politics.

And obviously Sir Bob Mahuta was very important – as were other Tainui people I grew up with when I moved to the King Country. We were on Tainui land so increasingly I met more of them. And one of my good friends and neighbours at Te Kūiti was the Labour minister Koro Wetere. Sir Hepi Te Heuheu was also an extraordinary man and a wonderful leader.

So, no single person was my mentor. But what I found was that they were all generous and fair in their observations about what could or couldn't be achieved. I don't recall any of them asking for something unreasonable.

In fact, it was Graham Latimer who, early on, advised me to be careful: 'Jim, make sure you don't create another grievance in solving a grievance.' I thought that was very wise.

The great news is that the fears that some had – like boats being locked out of Taupō, and people not being allowed in the Urewera – well, none of that has transpired. So the fears that some advanced from the fringes of politics about the terrible consequences – they've all been proven false.

What's your understanding of rangatiratanga or Māori sovereignty?

It's a challenging concept. And I have unsettled some people by suggesting that we should choose the Tino Rangatiratanga flag. It's a nice design in my view. And it reaches back into the history of New Zealand in a way that nothing else can. But I don't think that's going to happen, even though I support changing the flag.

MĀMARI STEPHENS
THE ONLY MĀORI IN THE ROOM

Māmari Stephens (Te Rarawa, Ngāti Pākehā) is a senior law lecturer at Victoria University of Wellington. This piece was published in September 2016.

I had one of those 'only Māori in the room' moments recently. I have a lot of those. These moments don't offend me. I work in mainstream tertiary education, I'm Māori and I profess to know something about things Māori. So what did I expect? Despite all that, these moments can be awkward.

I was in a meeting about a research funding proposal with very clued-up academics from various faculties. The heads swivelled in my direction as I'm asked my opinion on what I think the best direction for Māori would be, in regard to X or Y of the proposal.

There is a pause. Expectations hang heavy in the air. The words I say are to be weighed and perhaps given a weight disproportionate to their value. Or perhaps the reverse.

Sometimes, in moments like these, I can feel my cheeks flame. Sometimes, blind panic threatens to set in. On this occasion, however, I just snorted, laughed and said: 'Well, I don't know!' I may even have thrown my hands in the air.

That's usually how it is. I really don't know what Māori need, what Māori want, what direction would be best for Māori – how best to cater to, provide for, uphold and respect all things Māori. I have no portal into the Māori hive-mind. I take educated guesses in context. That's all I can ever do.

Of course, a lot of things have had to happen for me to have been the only Māori in that room. The absence of other senior Māori academics weighs more on me than does the cumulative weight of Pākehā expectation. There has been recent research done on the experience of senior Māori and Pasifika academics, which gives us some insight into why this is. Suffice to say, my experiences are hardly isolated, as a member of the 6 per cent of the academic workforce who identify as Māori.

Actually, my ruminations headed in a different, but related, direction. Because I'm not just assumed to be an ethnic representative of a people or peoples at moments like this. I'm expected to be a proponent of, and knowledgeable in, Māori culture to some degree.

Ah, culture. You marvellous double-edged sword, you.

After my meeting, I came home to a Facebook post that underscored the deep ambivalence I have towards our dominant notions of Māori culture. It was from an article outlining recent efforts being made to get young Māori into information technology:

Computer graphics company Animation Research's founder Ian Taylor [Ngāti Kahungunu, Ngāpuhi] said the lack of Māori engagement in ICT was disappointing, as in his experience when Māori got their hands on technology they adapted very quickly.

'I believe that Steve Jobs, he didn't realise it – but he designed the iPad for young Māori. It wasn't in our DNA to use paper and pen, never has been. We use our hands, we carve, we tell stories. We're great storytellers and technology has allowed us to engage in that way.'

Reading this reminded me of another such moment in 2014 and another public statement from the prominent Māori educator Terehia Channings, of the recently closed Turakina Māori Girls' College. Speaking on the benefits of kapa haka for kids, she said (and I'm paraphrasing here): 'Well, Māori are practical people. We have problems with maths and science, we learn best with our hands.'

In both cases – and you don't have to search too far to find other such presumptions bubbling up among friends and whānau – an ossified understanding of Māori culture is held up and venerated.

Māori people are practical. We make things and do things. We tell stories, we perform stories, but we don't write them down for others to read. And we probably don't read them either.

Forgive me if I take a moment off-screen to bash my over-educated head against a rather inviting red-brick wall.

Okay, I'm back.

I remember interviewing the actor and all-round extraordinary bloke Wi Kuki Kaa in 1992. He mused that people had often said to him that Māori were 'naturals' at acting, rugby and kapa haka.

'Nah,' he reckoned. In his view, if he had been raised in another family and in another culture, he would have been good at the things in those cultures. Māori weren't 'natural' at kapa haka. They were taught to be that way. There may be a genetic inheritance at work, but that can always be retooled in other cultures.

Culture is a human creation – that is all. It is the product of generations of people doing, saying, writing, thinking, eating, acting, singing, playing and being together. Rinse and repeat. There is no magic formula. There is no high-water mark of culture. There's no line we cross exactly when we know a cultural practice or a whole culture has died or forever changed. We just forget. And then we forget that we ever knew.

But culture, despite its blurred edges, performs an important function. Adherence to, or membership of, a culture (over and above mere ethnicity) grants us entry into something transcendent, beyond ourselves as individuals.

Membership of a minority culture in particular gives us access not only to that culture and to a meaningful cultural life, but the rights of protection that accrue to that culture at international and in domestic law. If there is no collation of practices, characteristics and products that can be identified as being of a given culture, then it cannot be protected.

On the one hand, we might tend to view culture as a mysterious unifying quality that marks out one set of human beings from another set of human beings. On the other hand, culture is a constraint. Once the hallmarks of a given culture are identified, reinforced and repeated, it becomes really difficult to challenge. Innovation and change pose huge risks to those who identify particularly with an indigenous or minority culture.

So, the very moment we call on culture to help us advance a position, identify solutions to political problems, create unity and affirm kinship, it bites us on the backside and orders us back into the box of our own bloody making.

There is no phrase that fills me with more dread than '*Māori are* …' And yet sometimes I use it. Because how else do we target and speak to Māori without identifying who we think Māori are? How do we employ Māori knowledge or seek it, without being open to seeing such knowledge is peculiarly Māori in the first place? How do we challenge Māori culture without first acknowledging that it exists?

I guess the answer is in common sense and moderation. We should reject essentialism – the idea that as Māori we're defined by an unchanging set of characteristics and behaviours – and the constraints it places on our evolution as a people. We should reject the position that sees no culture: that way lies cultural domination and oppression all over again.

And for the Māori in the room? She'd better be a good tightrope walker, is all.

GILBERT ENOKA
A WINNING FORMULA

Gilbert Enoka is the man many credit with the All Blacks' world-beating mental toughness and 'no dickheads' policy. He and his five brothers grew up in children's homes after their dad left their disabled mother to return to the Cook Islands. He talked to Dale Husband in June 2016 about growing up in an orphanage and the importance of being a good man.

Dale Husband: *E te rangatira, Gilbert. Thank you very much for talking to e-Tangata. Firstly, because we're notoriously nosy, maybe we could talk about your connections. And the Enoka name – where does it come from?*

Gilbert Enoka: Well, the Enoka name comes from Rarotonga. My father – Maro 'Jimmy' Enoka – was a born and bred Raro. He lived in Avarua. A lot of whānau there. And he travelled back and forth to New Zealand in his early years.

He came over here at forty and met my mother, Anna Eleanor Lynn, who was a Pākehā woman in Palmerston North. They had six children, of which I'm the youngest. I have five brothers. No sisters. Nine years between my oldest brother and me, so they were busy.

I didn't really know my father. My only real recollection of him was when he turned up at age sixty, basically saying: 'Here I am. Look after me.'

My mother was crippled. When my father left and went back to the islands, she couldn't look after us. So myself and my other five brothers were put into an orphanage. Into children's homes. There was one in Ōtaki, where I spent a good deal of my early life from eighteen months old. Then I got moved to Marton, to a home in Tutaenui Road. I stayed there until I was twelve years old. My brothers came and went. We didn't really spend a lot of time together as a family because we were at two different locations. Some were at Ōtaki.

I left the children's home at twelve and went back to Palmerston North to live with my mother, who had married my stepfather by then. I had these grandiose pictures of going back to this castle, this white palace. And I remember going into the house and seeing all these *Penthouse* pictures around the wall. The stepfather was pretty much ruled by alcohol. He had flagons on the table basically every morning when he got up.

So my vision of what life was like outside of the orphanage was absolutely shattered. I had to get out of there. So, at age sixteen, I left there and went down to Canterbury and went to university. I started studying physical education.

I bear no grudge against my mother or father. When I met my dad later, he was a simpler man. My mother, with all good intentions, tried to do the right thing. In hindsight, I had many helping hands at the orphanage. And a lot of things assisted me as I moved on through my journey.

I suppose, in a way, you were denied, not just an upbringing by your parents, but a cultural dimension to that upbringing as well. Do you have cause to resent that start?

That's a really good question. I've always felt an ihi and a specialness around Māori, and around the cultural aspect. I taught at Hillmorton High School and I would walk past the kapa haka group when they were performing. I just gravitated to them. I felt an umbilical connection.

At times, I feel like I missed out on a connection to that aspect of my whakapapa. I would love to have been brought up with the culture, to have had that nourishment. Because I think that would've just added to what I could bring, and enriched the talents I was blessed with. I experienced so many things around the way Māori and Pasifika do things. And they just seemed so normal, natural and special – and to have a deeper connection to how things are than in the Pākehā world.

Gilbert, I just assumed with a name like Enoka, that you were Māori. Did that happen to you a lot during the course of your early life?

Yes. Some of my brothers had Raro middle names, too. My oldest brother is Roger Maro. My third eldest brother is Bernard Teoe-ote-pai. As we got older, we began to value the specialness of those names, but in the early days, it was more of a challenge than a specialness. In those days, the bias towards the white man, the Pākehā, was strong. So we tended to get looked down on a little bit. Being in an orphanage, and obviously with the Raro background, there were some challenges. You learned how to fight. Which is a good thing.

Obviously, none of us are advocates for physical violence but I recall back in those times, young guys sort of had to stand up for themselves. You were raised in an orphanage, which most of us would look on as a hardship, and horrible, but maybe it wasn't quite like that. What would you say about those who cared for you for the better part of your first twelve years?

The people who cared for us were awesome. They were Brethren, a religious group, so it was based on doing a community good. The aunties and uncles, as we called them, were special people who gave up their lives to work inside the home. There probably would've been thirty to forty of us there at any one time. Their motives were always good.

We had an almost self-sufficient existence. We had animals. We killed our own sheep and meat. We had a huge vege garden. So we'd have to get up and do chores before we started the day. We came home and we did chores at the end of the day. Couldn't play sport. That was my only bugbear, because you had to come back after school and work. But, I learned a good work ethic. Was cared for really, really well.

I still remember the day I left, driving out of the gates. And I was actually in tears because I was leaving.

I don't have bad memories. Everything that was given to us, and directed to us, came out of a genuine sense of care. Hardship came more from the mental perspective – from seeing what other people had and what you didn't have. Those were the times I thought that there were certain people that lived in the world – and me. You thought you were different.

Did you lose contact with your brothers or are you a tight crew, still, to this day?

I was pretty much with my brother above me, Tony. We were at Ōtaki together and we were in Marton together. The other four of my brothers

174

were sort of split, so we didn't have much to do with them during that period. When they got to about fifteen, sixteen, my brothers left the orphanage.

They came and visited us. I can remember my oldest brother, Roger, who's now a professor in the States, coming to Ōtaki to visit us. There was a blocked toilet, and I can still remember, to this day, him unblocking the toilet and, as a reward, taking me and Tony for a walk down on the beach.

There were some special times. Once we left the orphanage, we remained extremely close. We met every Christmas. So we sort of had our collegial and communal childhood at a later age than most people. Through our twenties and thirties we'd Christmas together, we'd holiday together. We did everything together and remained very strong as a whānau.

What happened to the six lads? Did you all end up punching above your weight?

Pretty well. Roger is my eldest brother, and he paved the way. Very, very successful in his field. Probably the best in the world. I sometimes ask myself: 'How did you go where you went?' And I think part of me was just looking at Roger and seeing what he did. My second brother, John, died of cancer a couple of years ago. He owned his own furniture business in Palmerston North. My third brother, Bernard, he was a schoolteacher at Motueka High School. My next brother, Dudley, was CEO of the Yellow Pages, a billion-dollar company. He started off in Telecom licking stamps on telegram envelopes. Then my brother Tony is deputy principal at Waimea College in Nelson.

So you've got a group that's come out of a reasonable degree of adversity, and, as you say, punched above their weight and been really successful.

Hey, we all have our demons. You don't go through those sorts of experiences without getting scars. But we've worked pretty hard to get success. And we're all still with the first wives. All six of us. It's been an interesting journey for the Enoka whānau.

That last bit is a pretty remarkable stat in this day and age. Congratulations to you all. You went off initially looking at phys ed, but ended up doing psychology. Tell us why.

Well, I did physical education because I loved sport and everything it involved. I left my training course and went to teach at Hillmorton High School in Christchurch, which I loved. It was a low-decile school. So you had kids that didn't want to go to school. Kids that didn't want to go to class. Kids that didn't want to learn. They were people who had challenges, which I had a great affinity with, because my life had been filled with those sorts of things as well. So I loved my time there.

While I was there, I played volleyball. I ended up playing for New Zealand for ten years. Toured the world. And, at the same time, I coached volleyball at Hillmorton. Men's and women's. We actually got a national title at the school and a couple of runners-up.

I was a player-coach of our volleyball team and I was looking for ways to improve our performance. That led me down the track of the mind and how the brain works and how that can either assist or inhibit performance. I started exploring those dimensions and applying those principles to the teams I was coaching. I instantly connected with it, and it became a passion, which I pursued with vigour.

While I was at Hillmorton, Leigh Gibbs (former Silver Ferns' coach) was on the staff. She was also the coach of Canterbury Netball, and we had lots of conversations about what I was doing. So then I started working with Canterbury Netball. I was assistant coach for three years. And I worked with the Silver Ferns when Leigh was coach.

Wayne Smith, who was an All Black at the time, was working for Canterbury Sport and he would come round and sell sports equipment to the phys ed department. So I would sit down and have conversations with him. And I'd help him with his performance. He enjoyed it that much, that we began to work together. So we worked with

Canterbury B, Canterbury Sevens, New Zealand Sevens. Then with the Crusaders. Then on to the All Blacks.

I left Hillmorton because I loved psychology that much, I wanted to do a PhD. So I started studying that. Then, Chris Doig, who was the CEO of New Zealand Cricket at the time, was opening up the cricket academy, and he asked me to come and work with them. So I worked with the New Zealand cricket side. Had seven to eight years touring the world with them.

I fell into it through passion, initially. Connections, secondly. And then opportunity was probably the third one.

There have been many strong advocates, coaches, thinkers, looking for that top two inches, that little improvement in performance. The one-percenters. Who did you listen to, or read, or watch, that influenced or mentored you in your approaches to improving sports performance?

Well, in the early days, I was just thirsty for anything and everything. I read books and travelled to conferences. I remember when I was starting out, I used to have conversations with the late Laurie O'Reilly, who was the coach of the Canterbury University rugby team. He was ahead of his time as a coach. And I sort of said: 'Look, there's this conference in Portugal. I'd love to go to it.' It was the World Sport Psychology conference. I had a young family at the time, I was on a teacher's salary, so I just couldn't afford it. He pulled his chequebook out and wrote me a cheque for the airfares and accommodation. And he said: 'All you gotta do is come back and teach my team what you find.'

So, you know, you had people like that who were willing to help.

Things were going really good. We won national titles in volleyball. We had really good success in the cricket. We won at Lord's for the first time. We did some really wonderful things. With the Crusaders, we won four titles.

Then I went over to France in 2007 (with the All Blacks, for the Rugby World Cup), and we lost. We went over there expecting to win. Arrogant, probably. And we got bundled out in the quarterfinal. And I thought: 'Wow.' I was part of the problem, because I didn't have the answer to some of the things that we found most challenging at the time. A lot of people say the referee was the problem. We were more of the problem. I came back from that and said: 'Jeepers, you haven't got all the answers, mate. You need to get some help.'

So I formed a small group. There's a forensic psychiatrist here in Christchurch called Ceri Evans. A very, very smart man. There's an eighth dan martial artist called Renzie Hanham. And the three of us sat down, and I said: 'Look. I don't know the answers to this. We need to work on improving.' So we had conversations, and we became an advisory group to the All Blacks.

And, all of a sudden, my thinking took on a whole new dimension. It didn't just shift me. It catapulted me into a different sphere of understanding.

Since that day, I do look and read a bit, but I feel we're at the forefront and we're leading the world in a lot of areas that we don't share too much. Because we want to keep the intellectual property and we want to stay ahead of the curve.

One of the biggest questions that Graham Henry and Steve Hansen used to say to me is: 'Where are you going with this, Bert?' And I'd say: 'I don't know. But I know I'm heading in the right direction.'

I feel obliged to ask a little bit about motivating Māori and Polynesian players. You've heard the kōrero that our people don't have the patience for cricket. That we're not suited to individual sports. And we only like team sports. Has it been any more of a challenge, working out strategies to motivate our Māori and Pasifika men and women?

I think there's a couple of ways to answer that question. One thing I've learned is that you can't lump people into categories. To say that – because of this ability, because of this segment of society, because of this ethnicity – that these people are certain things.

I think some of our Polynesian brothers and sisters are constrained by two things. They're constrained a little bit by the tradition of respect because they're always trained to respect their elders and to look up to them. They don't challenge and question. But, sometimes, if what you hear ain't right, you've got to question and challenge your understanding. So we have to put structures in place that will allow or encourage people to do that.

The cultural dimension that exists within Māoridom and Pasifika is so much richer than anything I've ever encountered. And tapping into that, and leveraging that, is huge. I'd like to get some of our Māori and Pasifika people to dream bigger. Be bolder. To aim for higher clouds. Sometimes they're comfortable where they are now. And there's no gap between that and where they want to get to.

So, getting people to dream more and to aim big, and to question and probe – they're the sorts of things. For me, it's very individual. There are some challenges but if we can ignite and excite – boy. I always say: 'God didn't give everyone everything. You've got to find something yourself.' But I tell you what. Our Māori and Pasifika brothers and sisters, they've been given their fair share of the talent pool.

You'd be aware, too, that there's a school of thought that rugby and rugby league give licence to guys to remain adolescents into their thirties. But you push the line that good sportsmen can make good men, good fathers – and played a major part in transforming the All Blacks culture along those lines. Tell us about the 'no dickheads' policy that's associated with your thinking.

This is my sixteenth year in the All Blacks, so I've had a reasonable tenure. Longer than anyone. There's been 538 All Black tests over the last hundred years and I've been involved with 204 of them. So I've seen a lot.

And one thing I do know is that everyone is born with talent. But you won't realise that talent unless you become a good person. You can still be good. But I don't think you can be great, as defined by the talent you're given, unless you're a good person.

We've worked really hard on helping our people, our men and women, to become good people. Because, you do that, and then you realise that you're grateful as a human being for the talent you were given and the opportunity you were given. And, through that, you can then contribute and unleash that talent on the world.

Let's talk about the men, because that's who I mainly work with now. They're going to spend more of their lives as fathers, and as husbands, and as brothers, and as uncles, and as mates, than they are as All Blacks. We want to basically equip them with skill sets that allow them to become really positive contributors to the wider society.

We're on the countdown to wrapping up our kōrero. Who have you enjoyed working with? Not necessarily the best. But, of the many players you've come in contact with, whose growth have you enjoyed seeing most?

I don't think I can answer that in terms of a specific individual. I mean, the growth is so multi-dimensional.

You look at the mana of a Keven Mealamu, who is just such a humble, quiet, great man. His belief system's always been strong. But, it's seeing his growth, and the presence, and the mana and respect with which he's held by all races.

I look at a guy like Liam Messam, who was like a right-hand man for me, helping to connect our people with themselves, and with the bicultural nature of this country, and the multicultural nature of society. And building a brotherhood that becomes so much stronger than the individual parts.

You look at someone like Richie McCaw. I was in the shed when he played his first test. And in the shed when he played his 148th. The thing I loved most about that was, not only did we finish with a great All Black and a great All Black captain, of most significance is that he's a great man.

There's just so many dimensions to the people that come through this door. And they're enriched in so many ways, and they're growing in so many ways.

People slip up. They have mishaps. But, by and large, we have a management team that is hell-bent on assisting growth and ensuring that these men do become great citizens and great people in the community.

Has there been one particular event that stands out for you?

There's an old saying: *'Seldom is the last as good as the first.'* No one moment stands out, but many rise to the surface.

There were the early days, touring really hard and trying to win a volleyball championship. We lost three finals before we won our first national final.

There was working on *Kapa o Pango*, the new All Blacks' haka – this was after the All Blacks had lost an understanding of who they were as New Zealanders (in 2004, following their defeat to the Springboks). I spent a year working on that and putting together *Kapa o Pango*. And then unleashing that in Dunedin against the Springboks was so special.

You've got your grand slams. We've won three grand slams.

You've got the game in Ireland in 2013. We were down twenty-odd points and came back and won. We've got ourselves out of so many holes.

The two Rugby World Cups. The one most recently is reasonably special, because in 2011 we went from great to good. We played a semifinal really, really well. And then in the final, we just hung on. But in the last World Cup we went from great to great to great with the quarterfinal, semifinal and final.

So many great memories. And there's some tough times too. The losing in 2007. The early days when I was cutting my own track and people thought my area was witch-doctoring and wizardry, and if it didn't go well then it was all my fault.

You were acknowledged with the Order of New Zealand early in January 2016. Not something during the course of your life you would've given much thought to, but as a tohu for your efforts, and for those who helped to nurture you and support you through your life and no doubt your work, it must have been a special moment.

Like you say, it certainly wasn't something I sought out in life, but the moment it was received – and the impact it had on the whānau and the friends – it was just awesome. And receiving it from the governor-general, it was a fantastic honour. It was a very special occasion.

Looking ahead, what goals have you set yourself? What are you hoping to achieve for the rest of your life?

Good question. I started off as that shy wee boy in the orphanage, thinking I was really different. And sort of being indoctrinated with the understated, underdog nature – that way in which New Zealanders live their lives. And, in the last decade especially, the work I've done has helped forge a confidence that I have ability, and that I can achieve great things.

I'm looking to set the bar high. I'm pretty keen on working with the All Blacks to try and lock in a back-to-back-to-back Rugby World Cup. And I want to be there for my family, to support them and their endeavours.

I'll always chase and aim for the highest cloud, but at the same time I want to be a good father, a good husband, a good brother – and a bloody good mate.

MOANA JACKSON
FACING THE TRUTH
ABOUT THE WARS

Moana Jackson is a Wellington-based lawyer with a Ngāti Kahungunu and Ngāti Porou whakapapa. For many years he has been one of the country's leading thinkers, especially on the subject of the relationship between Māori and the Crown. He wrote this in September 2016, following the Crown's undertaking to 'commemorate' the nineteenth-century wars.

History always promises opportunities for truth. The debate generated by the petition from students of Ōtorohanga College to have the wars of the nineteenth century commemorated has led to the possibility of one such moment. The Crown announcement that a day will be set aside for commemoration appeared to indicate that the moment might be grasped, but unfortunately that may not be the case.

The announcement noted the day would be a chance for 'retelling of new histories that we have not heard before'. Yet the histories are not new to most Māori. The costs and consequences of the Crown decision to wage war against iwi and hapū have been a living history for generations.

The fact that there will at last be some other commemoration is welcome. But how will the wars actually be remembered?

Will there be an honest accounting of their brutality? And will there be any questioning of the power and wealth which the Crown acquired because of them – and which many Pākehā now take for granted?

Or will there simply be a revisionist and incomplete accounting that leaves the current power structures unchanged and unchallenged? What (or whose) history will the commemorations represent?

The history of war is never a simple remembering, because its truth always jostles uneasily with what people think about themselves and their past. This is especially the case in the wars of colonisation because they were merely the most extreme expression of the violence needed to take over the lands, lives and power of others.

Colonisation is an inherently brutal process and, in New Zealand, warfare was an inevitable part of the colonisers' need to establish their power in a land where they had never had any before. It was the raw acting out of a colonising will to dispossess – an unwarranted assault against innocents whose only offence was wanting to defend their homes.

In the Māori remembering of those wars, it is that defence of home which gives context to the never forgotten rape and aggression of every assault and every whim of the Crown's aggressive intent. It is the love of home which also gives meaning to the defence as both the expression and protection of tino rangatiratanga. It is found in a remembering in the land that still calls if people care to listen.

At Parihaka, it floats in the mist when it hangs low and hides the face of the maunga Taranaki, which the people there love so well. It sounds in the waiata which they still sing, and in the soft tapping of their poi or the steady beating of their drums. Each one remembers the promise of Te Whiti o Rongomai and Tohu Kākahi to cherish peace, while never forgetting that being peaceful in the face of invasion was a noble act of resistance.

Not far away, near Tauranga Ika, the remembering lies in what is now a quiet field and the terror-filled stories of playing children cut down by the colonisers' guns and sabres. Wi Te Tau Huata, who had been a chaplain in the Māori Battalion and knew the dread of war, once called that place 'he whenua pōuri': the land still wracked with grief because of what was done there. The field is now covered in soft grass, and the past has been furrowed deep in the land with each new planting. But the histories remain.

The same sad honesty and unequivocal defiance is found in other stories, too.

In Whakatōhea, the people do not flinch from the hostility of the wars, nor from the reality that they fought for the mana which they had been entrusted to hold for their mokopuna.

The original text on the memorial they erected at Te Tarata did not speak of someone else's nation building but of the stark facts of what happened there: *In memory to the 45 Ngāti Ira and others who were tragically slaughtered by cannon, the blade of the sword in the only cavalry charge in Aotearoa under the direct punitive scorched earth policy of the Crown during its raupatu and confiscation in October 1865.*

The painful courage of that honesty is now commemorated in nine pou embedded deep in the earth, as if they are drawing the stories up into the light.

Yet such stories are a recapturing of truth as much as a statement of record. For, once the wars had been fought, and written history replaced experience as the vehicle for understanding them, the colonisers tried to silence whatever iwi and hapū knew. Their causes and costs became a mere footnote in a story about building the new

New Zealand nation and the new Kiwi identity. It did not suit the colonisers' interests to question the unjustness of the wars, or the grievances they caused to iwi and hapū in terms of human suffering and the confiscation of millions of acres of land.

It suited them even less to question the overarching grievance of colonisation because to do so would have questioned the legitimacy (and the ethics) of both the wars and their claim to power.

Instead, truth and history were collapsed into a self-proclaimed innocence in which the takeover of the Māori world eventually became a takeover of historical memory. As a result, a strange silence fell over the wars, which clouded the truth like the smoke that had long faded over the battlefields.

Sometimes that silencing is described as a 'social amnesia', in which the past has slipped from the mind in the kind of almost accidental and blameless forgetting that occurs with the passage of time.

However, the wars never just wilted away as if by chance or a simple forgetting in the haze of long ago.

Like the other great misremembering, in which the Treaty of Waitangi is characterised as a voluntary giving up of iwi and hapū authority to the Crown, the stories of the war were consciously redefined in a way which flew in the face of Māori political and social realities.

Ceding mana or sovereignty in a treaty was legally and culturally incomprehensible in Māori terms – and the stories that eventually became the dominant narrative about the wars were similarly at odds with every belief iwi and hapū ever had about their authority and the grounds upon which they would take up arms to defend it.

There was no amnesia at play but a deliberate misremembering and renaming.

The renaming began with the 'Māori Wars', as if Māori were the belligerents and the colonisers were the aggrieved. Māori were described as 'rebels' or mocked on memorials to those who upheld 'law and order' against the forces of 'fanaticism and barbarism'. The fanatics and barbarians were the 'non-friendly' Māori who opposed the Crown, of course, and the 'law and order' was the authority the Crown wished to impose by destroying the law and order implicit in tino rangatiratanga.

The term 'Land Wars' then became popular, which unwittingly recognised that the taking of land was fundamental to the taking of power. However, it simplified the conflicts into the colonisers' struggle to become 'settlers' without acknowledging that in settling the land they were unsettling the people to whom it belonged.

But even the most persistent renaming could not entirely remove the reminders of what had been done, because the descendants of those who had been slaughtered were too close at hand. Renaming the past is best done when no one is around who lived the truth and most suffered its consequences.

Trying out the new Kiwi identity was thus a wayward and uncertain affair that always seemed caught between the cultural cringe of looking back to England as home and the nagging cringe of knowing what had happened here in someone else's home.

But with the invasion of Gallipoli in 1915, a morbid ANZAC fantasy provided a distant and safer source of identity. The sacrifice of a far-away battle became a sad but more comforting expression of 'Kiwi-ness' which was different from Englishness and unencumbered by the fatal proximity of the wars fought here. Gallipoli, of course, became a misremembering too, but its obsessive romanticism further silenced what had been done to Māori.

It is unfortunate that the recent commemoration discussions are based on the same misremembering. Their violence is less easily marginalised now because our people are more open to sharing the experience of a great wrong and less willing to accept the pulp fiction of those who committed the wrong.

However, while the Crown now acknowledges and 'regrets' the wars, it is also naming them as 'the wars which shaped the nation'.

This is just another misremembering because the assaults on iwi and hapū were always an attack on their political authority and thus their sense of independent nationhood. Just as the term 'settler' misrepresents the reality of dispossession, so the claim that the wars shaped the new nation ignores the fact that they purposefully misshaped the nations that were already here.

A proper commemoration of the wars means acknowledging all those different realities and accepting that they were neither the 'Māori Wars' nor the 'Land Wars' nor even 'the wars that shaped the nation'.

As some have noted, they were 'sovereignty wars', which more aptly recognises them as colonising wars to take power. To properly name them in that way is recognition that, in the end, any remembering of the pity of war is necessarily a political and historical act as well as a deeply human one. It requires an honest and even moral reckoning with the past, and a context which explains why certain things happened, and the consequences which flowed from them.

Because colonisation is the context, dealing with the wars must also be part of dealing with all that colonisation has done, including the constitutional and political power structures which it imposed. If a commemoration merely expresses regret for the painful wrong of the wars without having the courage to address those structures through a process of constitutional transformation, it is not a commemoration at all. It will simply be a deceit, rather like a burglar regretting the wrong but keeping the spoils.

It will not be easy to find that more honest commemoration, because historical truth can be discomfiting and seem impossible to change. It may even raise concerns about waking up dangerous sleeping dogs, but because the wars have never slept in the collective Māori consciousness, there is a greater risk in not addressing the need for a just remembering. This remembering would seek conciliation and an easing of the fretful reminders of a land that is not yet properly healed.

The Treaty held out an ineffable hope for such conciliation – and the memory of all those who suffered in the wars certainly deserves nothing less.

Only a commemoration which honourably remembers the past and paves the way to dealing with all that it has wrought can help us achieve that longed-for goal. Without it, the country will have forfeited this chance for truth in a history that is still with us.

MOANA MANIAPOTO
WHY WE'RE REO REFUGEES

Moana Maniapoto, staunch reo advocate, asks why, in 2016, she and other bilingual whānau have to go to such great lengths to find schools that teach the reo.

I'm a refugee. Apparently. I didn't know I was one until a Sunday newspaper told me.

When our baby was two, our family moved from our cool Grey Lynn apartment to a ramshackle whare on an Auckland west coast beach. Our friends in the city thought we'd lost the plot.

'You going all country on us, mate?'

Drama queens, we thought. We're only 45 minutes from Ponsonby Road, if you get a clear run.

For the first two years, we'd look up from repairing rotten floorboards and plugging leaks to savour the unbelievable ocean views. Sure, there was that northwestern motorway, but we didn't have to be anywhere in particular, at any particular time. We made new friends. We settled in. Even our city-slicker mates started dribbling out to us on a Sunday.

The funny thing about kids is they grow. I asked my neighbours about local kōhanga reo. They had no idea. We ended up at a puna, 30 kilometres away, run by the iconic Ereti Brown ('Nanny Letty'). We hit the peak-hour traffic every morning, thinking: *It could be worse.*

Ministry of Education figures released recently suggest that more than 81,000 students are commuting to out-of-zone schools each day, creating what critics call 'a culture of brown and white schools and rule-breaking' as parents try to get their kids into schools they're not zoned for. They call it 'white flight': parents trucking their kids into high-decile schools. In Auckland, 15 per cent of all children don't go to their local school.

That's us. The 15 per cent. Not the 'white flight' bit.

Every day, our (now) seven-year-old makes the 70-kilometre round trip to a suburb close to the one we originally lived in. We carpool with our Te Arawa relatives. It's a struggle. One day it took me eighty minutes to get to school. Our kids get good marks for attendance, but a fail for punctuality.

According to the *Sunday Star-Times* editorial, our families are part of the 'refugee flood based not in deprivation, but in ignorance'. Not so. We have two perfectly good, well-resourced schools less than 10 kilometres away from us, with excellent ERO reports. They just don't work for bilingual whānau.

Three years ago, I set up an appointment with the principal of our lovely local school.

'Our daughter is currently in a total immersion situation,' we said to the principal. 'How can your school support her learning?'

'We have excellent English remedial programmes,' he replied.

Come again? Maybe I needed to reframe that question.

'There's nothing wrong with her English,' I said. 'She's bilingual. How can *we* help *you* to support her reo?'

There was a pause.

'Well,' he said. 'There isn't really enough community interest in the Māori language.'

Not true. I'd talked to parents who had lobbied to get the language taught but couldn't gain traction.

'It's an official language,' barked The Father.

'It's the right of all kids, not just Māori, to learn te reo,' said I.

He smiled. We didn't feel the love.

We had visions of our little warrior princess fresh out of the warm embrace of Nanny Letty, now feeling like the odd one out. Our baby is not going to *that* school, muttered The Father. So we set up an appointment with the next closest school.

They had bilingual signage and a welcoming principal who fetched us coffee. Things were looking up. I asked him whether a Māori-speaking child would be seen as an asset or a liability.

'An asset!' he replied. 'I'd be lying if I said we can support your daughter's language needs but we would honestly welcome any help with the Māori curriculum you can give us.'

He took us on a guided tour of his little country school. It was festooned with notices about an upcoming lamb and calf day. Kids yelled out: 'Kia ora, sir!' We loved it. But we didn't have a lamb or a calf, just one Māori-speaking four-year-old and a sinking feeling.

It was 2013. We lived in the Supercity. Māori is an official language of New Zealand. There are plenty of flash jobs available to Māori speakers.

Yet Māori was not offered in any substantial way at our two local schools.

What were our options? We could put all our energy into joining other families to lobby for reo in the first school, or help transform the second school. Either process would take years. It was tempting to work alongside the keen principal but we'd already invested four years speaking only Māori to our kid. We needed backup. And we needed it now.

So we became refugees.

We followed our friends Scotty and Stacey Morrison to Westmere Primary. It had a bilingual unit and a waiting list. My family lives so out of zone that the administration office sent their reply to my (grovelling) letter to Muriwai. In *Gisborne*.

The Morrisons had the same experience as us. They are the go-to-for-reo people in Auckland for many whānau and had offered their considerable expertise and resources, along with thirty very keen parents, to a local school. But the headmaster 'couldn't muster the interest'.

Eighteen years had passed between enrolments of my two children into primary schools. My eldest went through kōhanga, then kura, in Māngere. I just assumed that in 2016, mainstream schools across Auckland would be a lot more sorted with the language. I was wrong.

In the last three years, the principal in the first school has defrosted somewhat, due to the efforts of some parents. The teachers are keen but need someone to implement the Māori curriculum. My mate has had to fend off a suggestion that she, being Māori and passionate, should take up the position.

She's aghast. It's not like anyone would expect another parent to manage the English curriculum of a school, just because they're Pākehā. Meanwhile, her daughter is being encouraged to learn Spanish.

Māori needs to be compulsory in all schools. But, first, we need a good, solid plan. As well as a concerted effort to train up more reo teachers, we need all principals to pass a Warrant of Fitness on reo and culture *before* they get the top job. When schools are ready, they need resource options tailored for their needs and those of their community.

We need reo programmes, digital and on TV – stuff that will excite and engage toddlers and tweenies. To get a frequency or licence, every single radio and TV station needs a WOF for pronunciation for all presenters and advertisements. And an annual renewal. As Stacey says, it's about professionalism. I'd call it a Treaty obligation, too.

And while we're at it, let's bring in a Māori-language music quota, too, and whack up bilingual signage everywhere. Good on MOTAT and Countdown for leading the way on that. And good on Rotorua for showing other cities how an official language can be normalised in an urban centre.

One of the most poignant moments our family has had was when my son was about five, and a waitress at Denny's spoke to him in Māori. The look of utter surprise and delight on his face makes me teary thinking of it.

Last week, I overheard a stranger speaking Māori to his boy as I was strolling through the Redwoods. It was unexpected in a setting outside the school, marae and home, but felt so natural.

Many families are embracing te reo. Our daughter's teacher and the head of our bilingual unit are fluent speakers and gifted teachers. They are Pākehā.

But these kids of ours keep on growing, so we parents have to keep on plotting, and compromising. Change will only come about through inspired leadership, in schools and across every sector.

We need to normalise te reo Māori.

Like most refugees, we don't want to be part of the flight. We want to come home.

ACKNOWLEDGEMENTS

The *e-Tangata* project is blessed to have many allies and kindred spirits who have given, and continue to give, their time and skills to the cause.

It also owes a huge debt of gratitude to The Tindall Foundation for its financial and moral support – and for understanding how important it is to the health of our country to support a strong Māori and Pacific media presence.

ABOUT THE EDITORS

Tapu Misa is a former reporter, feature writer, columnist (for the *New Zealand Herald*) and editor who was born in Samoa and grew up in Wellington. Gary Wilson grew up on a farm near Pukekohe, where he lives still. He's been a teacher, journalism trainer and editor since he began as an *Auckland Star* cadet reporter more than sixty years ago.

Together with broadcaster and te reo champion Stacey Morrison (Ngāi Tahu, Te Arawa), Tapu and Gary form the Mana Trust, which oversees *e-Tangata*.

About BWB Texts

BWB Texts are short books on big subjects: succinct narratives spanning history, memoir, contemporary issues, science and more from great New Zealand writers. All BWB Texts are available digitally, with selected works also in paperback. New Texts are published monthly – please visit www.bwb.co.nz to see the latest releases.

BWB Texts include:

Hopes Dashed?: The Economics of Gender Inequality
Prue Hyman

Safeguarding the Future: Governing in an Uncertain World
Jonathan Boston

The Stolen Island: Searching for 'Ata
Scott Hamilton

The Post-Snowden Era: Mass Surveillance and Privacy in New Zealand
Kathleen Kuehn

The Bike and Beyond: Life on Two Wheels in Aotearoa New Zealand
Laura Williamson

Late Love: Sometimes Doctors Need Saving as Much as Their Patients
Glenn Colquhoun

Three Cities: Seeking Hope in the Anthropocene
Rod Oram

Playing for Both Sides: Love Across the Tasman
Stephanie Johnson

Complacent Nation
Gavin Ellis

The First Migration: Māori Origins 3000BC – AD1450
Atholl Anderson

Silencing Science
Shaun Hendy

Going Places: Migration, Economics and the Future of New Zealand
Julie Fry & Hayden Glass

The Interregnum: Rethinking New Zealand
Morgan Godfery (ed)

Christchurch Ruptures
Katie Pickles

Home Truths: Confronting New Zealand's Housing Crisis
Philippa Howden-Chapman

Polluted Inheritance: New Zealand's Freshwater Crisis
Mike Joy

Wealth and New Zealand
Max Rashbrooke

Why Science Is Sexist
Nicola Gaston

Towards a Warmer World: What Climate Change Will Mean for New Zealand's Future
Veronika Meduna

The Edge of Life: Controversies and Challenges in Human Health
Mike Berridge

Out of the Vaipe, the Deadwater: A Writer's Early Life
Albert Wendt

No Country for Old Maids?: Talking About the 'Man Drought'
Hannah August

Time of Useful Consciousness: Acting Urgently on Climate Change
Ralph Chapman

Generation Rent: Rethinking New Zealand's Priorities
Shamubeel & Selena Eaqub

Haerenga: Early Māori Journeys Across the Globe
Vincent O'Malley

On Coming Home
Paula Morris

Ruth, Roger and Me: Debts and Legacies
Andrew Dean

The Struggle for Sovereignty: New Zealand and Twenty-First Century Statehood
Margaret Wilson

The Child Poverty Debate: Myths, Misconceptions and Misunderstandings
Jonathan Boston & Simon Chapple

The Piketty Phenomenon: New Zealand Perspectives
Various

Barefoot Years
Martin Edmond

New Myths and Old Politics: The Waitangi Tribunal and the Challenge of Tradition
Tipene O'Regan